The Bahá'í Faith:
Teachings, History, and Practices

Shahin Vafai

Palabra Publications

Palabra Publications
7369 Westport Place
West Palm Beach, Florida 33413
U.S.A.
1-561-697-9823
1-561-697-9815 (fax)
books@palabrapublications.info
www.palabrapublications.com

Photo credits: Pages 41, 44, 48, 51, 54, 72 and 79
Copyright Bahá'í Media Bank http://media.bahai.org.
Pages 70–71 by Ryan Lash.

CONTENTS

INTRODUCTION

The Bahá'í Faith is a world religion. Since its birth over a century and a half ago, it has taken root in more countries than any other religion except Christianity.[1] Its more than five million followers are found in some 100,000 localities around the world and represent nearly 2,100 ethnic, racial, and tribal groups. Its literature has been translated into over 800 languages. Its local institutions have been established in more than 10,000 communities. And its social and economic development projects operate in more than 100 countries. The worldwide Bahá'í community may well be the most diverse, organized body of people on the planet.

That people of nearly every ethnic, racial, and religious background have been attracted to the Bahá'í teachings confirms the vision of unity taught by the founder of the Bahá'í Faith, Bahá'u'lláh (pronounced "Ba-Ha-O-La"). In the nineteenth century, Bahá'u'lláh proclaimed that he was the bearer of a new revelation from God and the one promised by the

---

[1] *2002 Britannica Book of the Year* 302 (Encyclopaedia Brittanica, Inc. 2002) (identifying the number of countries in which each religion has "a numerically significant and organized following"):

Religion	No. of Countries
Christianity	238
Bahá'í Faith	218
Islam	204
Judaism	134
Buddhism	126
Hinduism	114

religions of the past. Christians, Muslims, Jews, Hindus, Sikhs, Zoroastrians, and Buddhists who have embraced the truth of the Bahá'í Faith have been attracted by its unifying principles. These principles include: there is only one God; all of humanity are children of God; and God has provided spiritual education for humanity through one process — the succession of the world's great religions. People of faith and those of no faith, the mystically-oriented and the practically-minded have been attracted to this belief system, which is spiritual at its core, yet scientific in its methods. They have appreciated the way it addresses their personal spirituality as well as the promotion of a just and peaceful society.

The growth of the Bahá'í Faith is remarkable not only because of the diversity of humanity that has responded to its message but also because it has spread despite continuous and severe persecution since its birth in Persia in 1844. The Faith's forerunner was publicly executed; its founder was subjected to 40 years of exile and imprisonment; its chief promoter was deprived of freedom for nearly half a century; and more than 20,000 of its early followers — men, women, and children — were put to death for their beliefs. In spite of such opposition, and at times because of it, the Bahá'í Faith has steadily spread to nearly every country in the world.

This text offers a brief introduction to the teachings, history, and practices that have aroused such a universal response. An exact and thorough description of the religion founded by Bahá'u'lláh is not possible here given that his writings constitute the equivalent of nearly 100 volumes. However, the following discussion quotes extensively from the Bahá'í sacred writings so that the reader may, to the extent possible, explore the Faith's teachings in their pure form. It is hoped that this introduction will provide a glimpse into the vision that has inspired millions of people worldwide.

CHAPTER 1

Learning about God:
The Role of the Divine Manifestations

This is the changeless Faith of God,
eternal in the past, eternal in the future.

– BAHÁ'U'LLÁH

Knowing God

What can one learn about God? And how can such knowledge be gained? These are among the most important questions on the path of spiritual search. The writings of Bahá'u'lláh offer answers to these profound questions.

Bahá'u'lláh taught that God is eternal, omniscient, and conscious of His creation. God's signs and attributes are reflected in creation, but the essence of God is unseen, inaccessible, and unknowable to human beings. Because God is unlimited and infinite, but the human mind is limited and finite, human beings cannot "comprehend the eternal, unmanifest Creator." Just as a painting lacks the capacity to understand the artist who painted it, so it is not possible for humanity to understand the essence of God, the Creator of all.

The Bahá'í scriptures explain that because we as human beings cannot directly access and know God, He has in each age sent a pure and stainless soul who has acted as an intermediary between God and humanity. God has provided this connection to Himself because of His love for humanity. These intermediaries (or "Manifestations of God") have included, for example, such historical figures as Moses, Jesus, Muhammad, and Bahá'u'lláh. They have been the founders of the world's great religions. The Manifestations are God's representatives — "mirrors that truly and faithfully reflect the light of God." While God's essence will forever remain unknowable to the human mind, God's qualities — such as love, mercy, knowledge, and power — may be known through the Manifestations who perfectly reflect these divine attributes: "In the Manifestation of God, the perfectly polished mirror, appear the qualities of the Divine in a form that man is capable of comprehending."

The analogy of the sun shining in a mirror helps to explain the relationship of God, the Manifestation, and humanity. God is like the sun, which is the source of life but which can never be closely approached or fully understood by any human being. The Manifestation of God is like a perfectly polished mirror that reflects the sun's light. Just as by turning toward the mirror, one is able to see the image of the sun, by turning toward the mirror of the Manifestation, one is able to see the spiritual image of God. In the Bahá'í view, this is what Jesus Christ meant when he declared that the Father was in him, namely, that "the reality of that eternal Sun had become reflected in its glory in Christ...."

Because each one of the Manifestations is the way that connects this world with the realm of God, whoever recognizes the Manifestation has recognized God. And because the infinite nature of God cannot be encompassed by the finite human mind, God "can never be known except through His Manifestation." An understanding of the role played by the Manifestation of God as the only direct link between God and humanity offers fresh insights into such scriptural statements as, "I am the way, the truth, and the life: no man cometh unto the Father, but by me." Such passages, which appear in the scriptural traditions of the world's religions, can come to be understood as more than claims of exclusive salvation. They can been seen as profound statements about the means by which humanity can know God — through the Manifestation who appears in each age. "Therefore, if man attains to the knowledge of the Manifestations of God, he will attain to the knowledge of God; and if he be neglectful of the knowledge of the Holy Manifestations, he will be bereft of the knowledge of God." The Manifestations have always been God's representatives and mouthpieces on earth, so their word is the word of God, their commandment is the commandment of God, and their prohibition is the prohibition of God.

The Manifestations of God as Divine Educators

According to the Bahá'í teachings, "The purpose of the appearance of the Manifestations of God is the training of the people." God sends the Manifestations to humanity to educate souls and to bring about a transformation in the character of mankind. As history shows, the Manifestations have often appeared and delivered their message among people who were either fast declining or had already reached the depths of moral and spiritual degradation. In other words, God sends His Manifestations to the world when people have moved away from God. For example, at various times in history, religion — or, more precisely, the corruption of religion — has caused conflict, division, fanaticism, and violence in the world. The Manifestations appear to again make known God's will and purpose and to restore religion to a positive, rather than destructive, force in society.

The Manifestations have transformed human beings by spiritually educating them, that is, by promoting the knowledge of God and furthering unity among people. So to discover whether an individual truly was a Manifestation of God, one must investigate the facts surrounding his life and history and examine whether he spiritually educated humanity. If such an individual were a true educator — if he trained an entire population, causing people to rise from the depths of ignorance to the heights of spiritual knowledge and conduct — that will offer evidence that he was a Manifestation of God.

For example, Moses was a divine educator. When Moses appeared, the tribes of Israel were in a state of disunity and misery as captives of the pharaohs. Through the divine law he revealed, Moses established unity among his people. He led them out of bondage into the Holy Land, uplifted them from ignorance and despair, and so trained them that they arose from a condition of captivity to one of honor. The Israelites became proficient in the sciences and arts and developed a civilization that became the envy of other peoples. The influence of Moses in shaping law and morality has endured for centuries.

Likewise, Jesus Christ, whom the Bible identified as the Son of God, was a divine educator of humanity. He appeared at a time when the Israelites had fallen from the heights of glory into a condition of spiritual, cultural, and moral decline. Jesus summoned all to righteousness, love, and spiritual rebirth. He ultimately sacrificed his own life that others might be edified by his teachings. Those who accepted and lived by his principles were uplifted and spiritually regenerated. Over time, the religion of Jesus unified various peoples and nations, bringing them together in fellowship and agreement. The teachings of Jesus brought under one banner such previously-warring groups as the Greeks, Romans, Egyptians, Assyrians, Chaldeans, and Phoenicians. In the past 2,000 years, the words and example of Jesus have touched and ennobled the lives of hundreds of millions of people around the world.

The spiritual and social transformation that Muhammad brought about in the Arabian peoples demonstrates that he too was a divine educator. In the seventh century, the tribes of Arabia were known for their barbaric cruelty, idol-worship, and immorality. Arab tribes were in an almost continual state of warfare with one another, killing, pillaging, and taking captive women and children. Such was the savagery of some Arabs that they even would bury their own infant daughters alive. Muhammad appeared among these people. He taught the Arab tribes to worship one God, to become united as one people, to take up arms only for defensive purposes, and to respect the rights of others, including Jews and Christians. Through Muhammad's training of the Arabs — who previously had been destitute of education and science — an impressive civilization emerged in the Middle East, North Africa, and Spain. While Europe was in the midst of the Dark Ages, the civilization Muhammad inspired became renowned for its scientific discoveries in various fields, including advancements in medicine and chemistry; the introduction of the Arabic numeral system; the establishment of universities attended by students from many nations; the founding of libraries containing hundreds of thousands of volumes; the translation of classical works of antiquity; the development of the arts; and the promotion of trade and commerce. Over time, many of these advances would be adopted by western countries.

Bahá'u'lláh is the most recent Manifestation of God who has spiritually educated large numbers of people. In the 1800's, he appeared in Persia (modern-day Iran), which had fallen from its past glory and become a most decadent society. Western scholars, diplomats, and travelers have described in detail the corruption, intolerance, and immorality of nineteenth century Persian society. Laws did not guide public affairs; instead, governmental officials ruled arbitrarily. Without resort to any system of justice, the accused were savagely punished and tortured — buried alive, blown from cannons, impaled, or dismembered. Government and commerce ran on bribes, which were open, shameless, and universal. Religious intolerance characterized daily life. Such was the religious prejudice among different faith communities in Persia that members of one religion could not associate in any way with those of another. The killing of those who held different beliefs was considered an act of worship. Rampant immorality was another feature of Persian society during this period. For example, moral values had declined to such an extent that religious leaders sanctioned and financially benefitted from a system of prostitution.

In such an environment, Bahá'u'lláh taught the principles of honesty, religious unity, and moral rectitude. Bahá'u'lláh instilled such a high standard of morality and trustworthiness in his followers that they became respected for their conduct and were often entrusted with positions of responsibility. Moreover, he succeeded in uniting Christians, Jews, Muslims, and Zoroastrians who began associating with one another as one family as a result of Bahá'u'lláh's teachings on religious unity. Despite systematic and ongoing efforts (which still persists today) by religious and governmental authorities in Persia to suppress the Bahá'í Faith, it has survived and grown. To date, several hundred thousand people have adopted Bahá'u'lláh's teachings in the land of his birth. Even greater numbers have accepted his principles in other countries, as members of previously antagonistic ethnic, racial, and religious groups have been unified by Bahá'u'lláh's teachings.

In sum, history has shown that the proof of the validity of a Manifestation of God is the transformative power of his words, the cultivation of virtues in the hearts and lives of his followers, and the appearance of divine education in the world.

It must be emphasized that the Manifestations of God are not simply smart leaders or influential philosophers. Rather, the nature of the Manifestation of God differs from that of ordinary human beings. The Manifestation of God is of a higher realm and has a perception and knowledge unlike that of any human being. Each of the Manifestations has embodied and revealed God's Word — they are the Word "made flesh." Moreover, they are endowed with divine knowledge and are not dependent upon learning acquired from others through schooling or personal study. While philosophers may offer intellectual training and may educate themselves and a limited number of other people, the Manifestations, through their innate knowledge, train and transform the human soul and have the capacity to educate entire civilizations. Even philosophers and other social leaders who have uplifted their people in various eras have been directly or indirectly influenced by the teachings of the Manifestations and have often acknowledged the inspiration provided by the Manifestations.

The Unity of the Manifestations of God and the Causes of Religious Differences

From the Bahá'í perspective, the appearance and teachings of the Manifestations of God are not random or divergent. Instead, the Manifestations are divine educators who have revealed God's message in an orderly, continuous, and progressive way. Their teachings are part of a single spiritual process — different stages in the development of one religion. According to the Bahá'í teachings,

> All these holy, divine Manifestations are one. They have served one God, promulgated the same truth, founded the same institutions and reflected the same light. Their appearances have been successive and correlated; each One has announced and extolled the One Who was to follow, and all laid the foundation of reality. They summoned and

invited the people to love and made the human world a mirror of the Word of God. Therefore, the divine religions They established have one foundation; Their teachings, proofs and evidences are one; in name and form They differ, but in reality They agree and are the same.

The appearances of the Manifestations of God are as the daily appearance of the sun. Each day bears a different name and date, but today's sun is the same as yesterday's. Similarly, the Manifestations of God differ in name and outward appearance, but they bring the same light of God to humanity. The rising and setting of the sun of God's Manifestations will continue indefinitely. While the light of the Manifestations is the same, each offers to humanity a measure of divine guidance that is fuller than any which an earlier and less receptive age could have received.

If there is unity among the Manifestations and if their teachings represent different stages of one religion, why then do the doctrines and practices of the world's great religions differ in key respects? The Bahá'í scriptures offer several explanations.

First, the Manifestations of God have each brought to humanity two types of teachings: essential, spiritual teachings and temporary, social teachings. The essential teachings concern spiritual virtues and divine qualities such as faith in God, the love of fellow human beings, justice, righteousness, trustworthiness, and humility. These are eternal commandments that will never be abolished. As such, spiritual teachings like the golden rule — treating one's neighbor as one wishes to be treated — appear in all of the world's major religions.

The second type of teachings brought by the Manifestations are social laws and regulations — concerning, for instance, marriage and divorce, forms of worship, or criminal penalties — that are subject to change according to the requirements of time and place. "For example, in the time of Moses divorce was conformable to the needs and conditions; Moses, therefore, established it. But in the time of Christ, divorces were numerous and the cause of corruption; as they were not suitable for the time, he made divorce unlawful and likewise changed other laws." Further,

> Other laws embodying drastic punishments were enacted by Moses — an eye for an eye, a tooth for a tooth. The penalty for theft was amputation of the hand. These laws and penalties were applicable to... the Israelitish people of that period, who dwelt in the wilderness and desert under conditions where severity was necessary and justifiable. But in the time of Jesus Christ this kind of law was not expedient; therefore, Christ abrogated and superseded the commands of Moses.

Therefore, the differences in the teachings of the great religions are, in part, due to the changing needs of humanity.

While the Manifestations are sent by God and reflect His light, each has been the bearer of a specific message and has had a definitely prescribed mission. God charges each Manifestation to best meet the requirements of the age in which he appears. Bahá'u'lláh likened the Manifestations to divine physicians whose task is to "heal the sickness of a divided humanity." He further commented, "Little wonder, then, if the treatment prescribed by the physician in this day should not be found to be identical with that which he prescribed before. How could it be otherwise when the ills affecting the sufferer necessitate at every stage of his sickness a special remedy?" "The skillful physician does not give the same medicine to cure each disease and each malady, but he changes remedies and medicines according to the different necessities of the diseases and constitutions." The divine remedy the Manifestation prescribes may well differ from age to age, depending on the spiritual and social ailments afflicting society at that time.

The Need for the Renewal of Religion

Another reason for the differences in beliefs among the followers of the world's religions is that, over time, the original teachings of the divine religions are altered or forgotten, and man-made ideas are introduced into practice. According to the Bahá'í teachings, the change in religion is similar to the progression of the seasons. The coming of a Manifestation of God is like the appearance of the spiritual springtime. During the spiritual springtime when the religion of God first appears, spirits are renewed, hearts are refreshed, and progress is achieved. Spring is followed by the fruitful summer when the law of God spreads, the divine teachings permeate the world, humanity becomes educated, and praiseworthy results are achieved. Summer, in turn, is succeeded by autumn during which growth stops and decline begins. During autumn, spirituality is changed, virtues are replaced by vices, holiness and purity disappear, and only the name of the religion of God and its outward form remain. Finally, religion's winter arrives: the coldness of ignorance envelops the world, the darkness of human error prevails, and people become indifferent, disobedient, inconsiderate, and base. However, "God leaves not His children comfortless, but, when the darkness of winter overshadows them," He sends another Manifestation who will usher in the "renewal of the blessed spring."

The Bahá'í scriptures also use the analogy of the planting of a new tree to convey how the religion of God is one religion, but must be continually renewed:

> ...the religions of God have been made manifest, one following the other, and each one of them

fulfilled its due function, revived mankind, and provided education and enlightenment.... As each succeeding Faith and Law became revealed it remained for some centuries a richly fruitful tree and to it was committed the happiness of human-kind. However, as the centuries rolled by, it aged, it flourished no more and put forth no fruit....

≈

This is why the True Gardener plants again an incomparable young tree of the same kind and species, which grows and develops day by day, and spreads a wide shadow in the divine garden, and yields admirable fruit. So it is with religions; through the passing of time they change from their original foundation, the truth of the Religion of God entirely departs, and the spirit of it does not stay; heresies appear, and it becomes a body with-out a soul. That is why it is renewed.

Bahá'u'lláh explained that the renewal of religion occurs about every thousand years. He declared that he ushered in a period of spiritual renewal as the latest Manifestation of God: "The Divine Springtime is come...."

Because God's revelation to humanity is continuous, Bahá'u'lláh did not claim to have brought the final revelation from God. He anticipated that, after the passing of at least one thousand years, God will again send humanity another Manifestation, who like all the previous Manifestations, will renew God's essential spiritual teachings and introduce social teachings needed at that time. Through this process, God will forever transmit His love and knowledge to humanity.

CHAPTER 2

Understanding Ourselves:
Human Nature, Life's Purpose, and the Afterlife

*...true life is not the life of the flesh
but the life of the spirit.*

– BAHÁ'U'LLÁH

The Three Aspects of Human Beings

Throughout religious history, the Manifestations of God have taught that life has a spiritual purpose. Bahá'u'lláh has reaffirmed the spiritual teachings of previous religions and offered new insights into the nature of human beings, the purpose of life, and the features of the afterlife.

According to the Bahá'í teachings, each human being has three aspects: a body, a mind, and a soul (or spirit). The human body has material form, is visible, and will physically disintegrate after death. By contrast, the human soul does not have material form, is invisible, and is immortal. The "mind forms a link between the soul and the body."

The Bahá'í scriptures shed light on the characteristics of the soul and the mind. The soul emanates, or comes forth, from God in the same way that writing emanates from a writer, speech from a speaker, or action from an actor — reflecting the qualities of its creator. As such, the soul is a sign of God.

Because the "soul is fashioned after the nature of God," it is pure and holy at birth. Afterwards, however, "individuals will vary according to what they acquire of virtues or vices in this world."

The soul comes into being with the conception of the physical body. But since the soul does not have physical qualities, it is not contained within the body. Rather, the soul is connected with the body as the sun is with a mirror turned towards it. Just as the light of the sun may be seen within a mirror (though the sun is not physically inside the mirror), the light of the soul is reflected within the body (though the soul is not physically inside the body). Given this relationship between the body and the soul, when the mirror of the body breaks — on account of death — the body will cease to reflect the light of the soul, but the soul will continue to exist.

Human beings have physical powers and outer senses in common with animals, yet the extraordinary power of the soul, as expressed through the mind, has enabled humanity to achieve what no animal is capable of achieving. The power of conscious reasoning has enabled humans to unravel mysteries of nature, to generate inventions, and to create art. This power of the soul is evident in the capacity of people to resist the restrictions of nature. Alone among living creatures on earth, human beings are not limited by all of nature's constraints. The human body, for example, is not naturally equipped to fly, but we have invented aircraft to allow us to soar through the sky. Our bodies lack the physical ability to swim vast distances, but we have invented ships that permit us to traverse the ocean. And although we have limited strength to lift or transport objects, we have created tools and machines that move tons. The human capacity to overcome the restrictions of nature demonstrates that there lies within each human being a special power: the human soul.

Material and Spiritual Natures of Human Beings

In light of their makeup, human beings have two natures: the physical (or lower) nature and the spiritual (or higher) nature. Signs of both these natures are found within human beings.

Our lower nature acts according to the dictates of the physical world. This lower nature expresses such dark qualities as "antagonism, hatred and selfish struggle for existence,… jealousy, revenge, ferocity, cunning, hypocrisy, greed, injustice and tyranny." All human imperfections are born of the lower, physical nature. Those whose lives are dominated by their lower nature "have no thought beyond earthly possessions and manifest no desire save the passions of this fleeting, mortal existence." The lives of such people

are solely occupied with the things of this world; their minds are so circumscribed by exterior manners and traditional interests that they are blind to any other realm of existence, to the spiritual significance of all things! They think and dream of earthly fame, of material progress. Sensuous delights and comfortable surroundings bound their horizon, their highest ambitions center in successes of worldly conditions and circumstances!… Like the animal, they have no thought beyond their own physical well-being.

By contrast, "Every good habit, every noble quality belongs to man's spiritual nature," which transcends the material world and is connected with God. Our spiritual nature expresses divine qualities such as love, mercy, kindness, truth, justice, knowledge, wisdom, and sacrifice for the well-being of others. This spiritual nature also reflects intellect, comprehension, and the power to penetrate the truths of existence.

Because human beings have both a physical and a spiritual nature, we have the power to do good or evil. When the spiritual nature dominates the physical, the spiritual purpose of life is fulfilled. Such persons have freed themselves from the material world: "They live in the world but are not of it, their thoughts being continually in the world of the spirit. Their lives are spent in holiness, and their deeds show forth love, justice and godliness."

But if an individual's spiritual qualities are never used, they become atrophied, enfeebled, and ultimately incapable of functioning. When a person focuses only on his material nature, the material qualities "become terribly powerful — and the unhappy, misguided man, becomes more savage, more unjust, more vile, more cruel, more malevolent than the lower animals themselves." Such individuals "plan to work evil, to hurt and to destroy; they are entirely without the spirit of Divine compassion, for the celestial quality of the soul has been dominated by that of the material."

The Bahá'í teachings on the twofold nature of human beings help to explain the broad range of behaviors and characters among people, from those who embody goodness and selflessness to those who are filled with hatred and selfishness. Through the exercise of free will to develop his or her spiritual or material qualities, each person has the potential to be either the light of the world or its darkness: "God Himself does not compel the soul to become spiritual. The exercise of the free human will is necessary."

Being spiritually inclined does not mean forsaking all material possessions, foregoing the pleasures of this world, or forgetting about the practical necessities of life. One can have possessions, yet not be possessed by them. One can enjoy the physical pleasures of this earthly life, but not make them the object of life. And one can, and should, maintain one's health and attend to life's practical needs without being obsessed with worldly necessities. As the Bahá'í teachings point out:

> Life is a load which must be carried on while we are on earth, but the cares of the lower things of life should not be allowed to monopolize all the thoughts and aspirations of a human being. The heart's ambitions should ascend to a more glorious goal, mental activity should rise to higher levels! Men should hold in their souls the vision of celestial perfection, and there prepare a dwelling-place for the inexhaustible bounty of the Divine Spirit.

From the Bahá'í perspective, one may partake of the benefits of the material world so long as those benefits do not interfere with one's relationship with God. Bahá'u'lláh explained: "Should a man wish to adorn himself with the ornaments of the earth, to wear its apparels, or partake of the benefits it can bestow, no harm can befall him, if he alloweth nothing whatever to intervene between him and God, for God hath ordained every good thing, whether created in the heavens or in the earth, for such of His servants as truly believe in Him."

The Purpose of Life and the Role of the Manifestations of God

If the object of life is to develop one's spiritual capacities and qualities, how does one achieve such spiritual growth? According to the Bahá'í teachings, the Manifestations of God are the divine educators who show humanity the path of spiritual growth. The Manifestations teach us about the purpose of life and prescribe those actions that are conducive to the development of the spirit.

Reinforcing the teachings of previous Manifestations about the purpose of life, Bahá'u'lláh taught that God has conferred on the human soul the capacity to know and love God. Indeed, God has made the human soul "a mirror of His own Self." Therefore, the purpose of life lies in knowing God and reflecting His divine qualities. As discussed earlier, the essence of God is unknowable, so acquiring the knowledge of God means learning about and embodying divine qualities such as love, justice, and forgiveness. This echoes the Biblical teaching that God created human beings in His image: "Let us make man in our image, after our likeness...." As explained in the Bahá'í teachings,

> It is self-evident that the image and likeness mentioned do not apply to the form and semblance of a human being because the reality of Divinity is not limited to any form or figure. Nay, rather, the attributes and characteristics of God are intended. Even as God is pronounced to be just, man must likewise be just. As God is loving and kind to all men, man must likewise manifest loving-kindness to all humanity. As God is loyal and truthful, man must show forth the same attributes in the human world. Even as God exercises mercy toward all, man must prove himself to be the manifestation of mercy. In a word, the image and likeness of God constitute the virtues of God....

The Manifestations help humanity fulfill life's spiritual purpose by summoning everyone to "truthfulness and sincerity, to piety and trustworthiness, to resignation and submissiveness to the Will of God, to forbearance and kindliness, to uprightness and wisdom." Like divine gardeners who prepare the earth of human hearts and minds, the Manifestations educate humanity, uproot materialistic weeds, and transform spiritually barren land into gardens where fruitful trees grow. They do all this by enjoining actions that lead to spiritual growth and discouraging, or even prohibiting, conduct that retards spiritual development. Bahá'u'lláh declared that the Manifestations "have forbidden men from following whatsoever might cause them to stray from the Truth, and have commanded them to observe that which will draw them nearer unto Him Who is the Almighty, the All-Loving." Through the teachings of the Manifestations, "every man will advance and develop until he attaineth the station at which he can manifest all the potential forces with which his inmost true self hath been endowed." Because the ultimate aim of every soul should be to achieve spiritual excellence, the soul achieves happiness by striving to develop spiritually:

> ...the honor of the human kingdom is the attainment of spiritual happiness in the human world, the acquisition of the knowledge and love of God. The honor allotted to man is the acquisition of the supreme virtues of the human world. This is his real happiness and felicity.

If God's Manifestation is the source of truth and establishes the way toward spirituality, then each person should strive to follow this path, which consists of accepting and applying the teachings of the Manifestation. Thus, from the Bahá'í perspective, attaining the condition of heaven depends on two factors: first, faith in God's Manifestation in the age in which he appears and, second, good deeds. A person cannot claim to truly believe in God through His Manifestation if that belief is not translated into good works — the living of a noble and spiritual life in accordance with the Manifestation's teachings. Similarly, it is incomplete to lead a life of good works but reject the source of that goodness. As the Bahá'í scriptures declare, "faith compriseth both knowledge and the performance of good works."

Preparing for the Afterlife

Bahá'u'lláh explained that the Manifestations of God "have been sent down for the sole purpose of guiding mankind to the straight Path of Truth." Further, "The purpose underlying Their revelation hath been to educate all men, that they may, at the hour of death, ascend, in the utmost purity and sanctity and with absolute detachment to the throne of the Most High."

Because the soul is eternal, the purpose of life in this physical world is to prepare the soul for the next world. Although we cannot, while in this world, understand the precise nature of the afterlife, Bahá'u'lláh has offered some glimpses of that world. He wrote that the "world beyond is as different from this world as this world is different from that of the child while still in the womb of its mother." The life of the embryo is confined and limited in comparison with the world it will soon enter. When an infant is born into this world,

> it finds that it has passed from darkness into a sphere of radiance; from gloomy and restricted surroundings it has been transferred to a spacious and delightful environment. Its nourishment was the blood of the mother; now it finds delicious food to enjoy. Its new life is filled with brightness and beauty; it looks with wonder and delight upon the mountains, meadows and fields of green, the rivers and fountains, the wonderful stars; it breathes the life-quickening atmosphere....

Similarly, when a person dies, his or her soul moves from this restricted, physical world to a liberated, spiritual realm. The soul transitions from darkness and uncertainty to light and reality. One is "freed from a world of sorrow, grief and trials to live in a world of unending bliss and joy."

Like the embryo that begins to fully see and hear after its birth, the human soul will attain spiritual sight and hearing after moving to the life beyond:

> When the human soul soareth out of this transient heap of dust and riseth into the world of God, then veils will fall away, and verities will come to light, and all things unknown before will be made clear, and hidden truths be understood.

> Consider how a being, in the world of the womb, was deaf of ear and blind of eye, and mute of tongue; how he was bereft of any perceptions at all. But once, out of that world of darkness, he passed into this world of light, then his eye saw, his ear heard, his tongue spoke. In the same way, once he hath hastened away from this mortal place into the Kingdom of God, then he will be born in the spirit; then the eye of his perception will open, the ear of his soul will hearken, and all the truths of which he was ignorant before will be made plain and clear.

The analogy of the embryo's development within the womb also helps to explain the purpose of this earthly life in relation to the next world. When in the womb, the embryo develops certain physical faculties that are primarily intended for use after birth. For example, in this world, the child needs eyes and ears; these are developed while in the womb. If the embryo does not develop all the essential, physical faculties while in the womb, the child will be physically impaired after birth. Likewise, the purpose of this life is to develop the spiritual faculties needed for the afterlife:

> That world beyond is a world of sanctity and radiance; therefore, it is necessary that in this world he should acquire these divine attributes. In that

world there is need of spirituality, faith, assurance, the knowledge and love of God. These he must attain in this world so that after his ascension from the earthly to the heavenly Kingdom he shall find all that is needful in that eternal life ready for him.... That is a world of love; the love of God is essential. It is a world of perfections; virtues, or perfections, must be acquired.

The Nature and Features of the Afterlife

When the body dies, the soul lives on. After the death of the body, the soul permanently leaves this material world and enters the spiritual world in which it can indefinitely advance.

Bahá'u'lláh explained that after its separation from the body, the soul retains its individuality and consciousness and "will continue to progress until it attaineth the presence of God." Because the next world is a spiritual world and does not have a material existence, it is beyond time and place. People who have passed on to the next world do not assume a physical form. Rather, they assume a heavenly form, which cannot be fully described or understood in this world. The nature of that spiritual world is different from and superior to this earthly life.

Just as the growth and development of the embryo become fully apparent only after the child is born, the results of human actions in this life will become revealed in the afterlife. Bahá'u'lláh wrote, "all men shall, after their physical death, estimate the worth of their deeds, and realize all that their hands have wrought." If the deeds carried out on earth did not have results in the world beyond, "the whole process would be irrational and foolish."

The soul who has "walked in the ways of God...will, assuredly, return and be gathered to the glory of the Beloved." That soul will find itself invested with honor and glory. And the pure, refined, and sanctified soul "will be endowed with tremendous power, and shall rejoice with exceeding gladness." As such, from the Bahá'í perspective,

> the rewards of the other world are the eternal life which is clearly mentioned in all the Holy Books, the divine perfections, the eternal bounties and everlasting felicity. The rewards of the other world are the perfections and the peace obtained in the spiritual worlds after leaving this world.... The rewards of the other world are peace, the spiritual graces, the various spiritual gifts in the Kingdom of God, the gaining of the desires of the heart and the soul, and the meeting of God in the world of eternity.

By contrast, the punishment of the next world consists in being deprived of the spiritual bounties of God.

Therefore, heaven and hell are not locations, but are conditions within our own beings. If a soul is in a condition of nearness to God, by recognizing God's Manifestation, then that soul is in a state of heaven, where paradise is God's love and the soul's heavenly home is reunion with God. By contrast, whoever has turned away from God, by failing to recognize His Manifestation, has condemned himself to the misery of remoteness, which is the condition of hell or utter nothingness. Bahá'u'lláh emphasized that any person who is spiritually born and is quickened by the spirit and teachings of God's Manifestation has "entered into the 'paradise' of the love of God."

CHAPTER 3

Building a Just, Peaceful, and Progressive Society:
The Principles of Unity

*So powerful is the light of unity that
it can illuminate the whole earth.*

– BAHÁ'U'LLÁH

Overview of Principles

God's purpose in sending the Manifestations to humanity is twofold: "The first is to liberate the children of men from the darkness of ignorance, and guide them to the light of true understanding. The second is to ensure the peace and tranquillity of mankind, and provide all the means by which they can be established." Therefore, in addition to aiding the individual to grow spiritually, the Manifestations of God promote the harmonious development of society. Bahá'u'lláh, like the Manifestations of the past, has revealed principles that will enable the establishment of a just, peaceful, and progressive society.

According to the Bahá'í teachings, achieving peace in the world involves much more than limiting nuclear weapons and ending particular conflicts. Taking such steps will not remove the root causes of war. People are ingenious enough to devise new forms of warfare and to use any available means, such as food, raw materials, terrorism, or the Internet, to attempt to inflict harm upon others. Real peace can be achieved only when humanity addresses the fundamental causes of conflict — including racial, religious, and national prejudices; the oppression of women; and economic injustice. Only when such underlying causes of war are remedied will disunity disappear and peace be attained.

The writings of Bahá'u'lláh present principles and concepts that attempt to remove the causes of conflict. Revolutionary when first taught more than a century ago, the teachings of Bahá'u'lláh remain the remedy for the ailments afflicting the world today. These principles and concepts include:

- The oneness of humanity
- The independent investigation of the truth
- Unity as the purpose of religion
- The harmony of religion and science
- The elimination of prejudices
- The equality of men and women
- Universal education
- Auxiliary international language
- Economic justice
- Universal peace through collective action

The Oneness of Humanity

The principle of the oneness of humanity is the cornerstone of Bahá'u'lláh's teachings. Addressing humanity, Bahá'u'lláh declared: "Ye are the fruits of one tree, and the leaves of one branch. Deal ye one with another with the utmost love and harmony, with friendliness and fellowship." This principle of the unity of mankind means: "All are the servants of God and members of one human family. God has created all, and all are His children. He rears, nourishes, provides for and is kind

to all. Why should we be unjust and unkind?" According to
the Bahá'í teachings,

> no one should glorify himself over another; no
> one should manifest pride or superiority toward
> another; no one should look upon another with
> scorn and contempt; and no one should deprive
> or oppress a fellow creature. All must be consid-
> ered as submerged in the ocean of God's mercy. We
> must associate with all humanity in gentleness and
> kindliness. We must love all with love of the heart.
> Some are ignorant; they must be trained and edu-
> cated. One is sick; he must be healed. Another is
> as a child; we must assist him to attain maturity.

As such, the oneness of humanity is both a principle
and a goal. It is a spiritual principle that science confirms.
Anthropology, physiology, and psychology recognize that there
is only one human species, although varied in appearance,
culture, and tastes. At the same time, unity is a goal toward
which humanity is evolving. But oneness is not sameness. The
Bahá'í Faith does not seek to establish uniformity, but a unity
in diversity:

> Consider the flowers of a garden.... How unpleas-
> ing to the eye if all the flowers and plants, the
> leaves and blossoms, the fruits, the branches and
> the trees of that garden were all of the same shape
> and color! Diversity of hues, form and shape,
> .enricheth and adorneth the garden, and height-
> eneth the effect thereof.

In like manner, diversity of culture, thought, and temperament
enriches the tapestry of human life as people of varied backgrounds offer their contributions to a united society.

The Independent Investigation of the Truth

One of Bahá'u'lláh's fundamental teachings is the independent investigation of the truth — that all should "see with their own eyes and hear with their own ears" and not blindly follow the beliefs of their ancestors and forefathers. Many in the world follow a set of religious beliefs, not because of personal investigation and thought, but because their parents were followers of that religion. From the Bahá'í perspective, belief should not be merely an accident of nature, dependent upon what family or region of the world one happens to be born into. Instead, belief should stem from the exercise of independent inquiry and free will: "God has created in man the power of reason, whereby man is enabled to investigate reality.… He has endowed him with mind, or the faculty of reasoning, by the exercise of which he is to investigate and discover the truth, and that which he finds real and true he must accept."

Unity as the Purpose of Religion

According to Bahá'u'lláh, the purpose of religion is to establish unity among the peoples of the world. In the 1800's, Bahá'u'lláh referred to religious fanaticism and hatred as a "world-devouring fire." Recent history has only confirmed the danger that Bahá'u'lláh anticipated. From the Bahá'í perspective, if "religion becomes the source of antagonism and strife, the absence of religion is to be preferred." "The purpose of a remedy is to heal and cure. If it be productive of worse symptoms, its absence or discontinuance is preferable." To overcome religious prejudices, Bahá'u'lláh counseled: "Consort with the followers of all religions in a spirit of friendliness and fellowship." Such association is conducive to promoting unity.

The Harmony of Religion and Science

Bahá'u'lláh also taught that religion must be in conformity with science and reason. He wrote that the rational faculty should be regarded as a sign of the revelation of God. "Intellect is, in truth, the most precious gift" bestowed by God upon humanity. "The sciences and arts, all inventions, crafts, trades and their products have come forth from the intellect of man." If religious belief and teaching are opposed to reason and principles of science, they are unworthy of acceptance. "Any religious belief which is not conformable with scientific proof and investigation is superstition, for true science is reason and reality, and religion is essentially reality and pure reason; therefore, the two must correspond." Further,

> Religion and science are the two wings upon which
> man's intelligence can soar into the heights, with
> which the human soul can progress. It is not pos-
> sible to fly with one wing alone! Should a man try
> to fly with the wing of religion alone he would
> quickly fall into the quagmire of superstition,
> whilst on the other hand, with the wing of science
> alone he would also make no progress, but fall into
> the despairing slough of materialism.

"If we say religion is opposed to science, we lack knowledge of either true science or true religion, for both are founded upon the premises and conclusions of reason, and both must bear its test."

The Elimination of Prejudices

Prejudice, whether religious, racial, patriotic, or political, is "the destroyer of human foundations and opposed to the commands of God." Bahá'u'lláh wrote: "The earth is but one country, and mankind its citizens." From the Bahá'í perspective,

> The earth has one surface. God has not divided this surface by boundaries and barriers to separate races and peoples. Man has set up and established these imaginary lines, giving to each restricted area a name and the limitation of a native land or nationhood. By this division and separation into groups and branches of mankind, prejudice is engendered which becomes a fruitful source of war and strife. Impelled by this prejudice, races and nations declare war against each other; the blood of the innocent is poured out, and the earth torn by violence.

The "cause of bloodshed and battle, strife and hatred throughout the past has been either religious, racial, patriotic or political prejudice," and "the root cause of prejudice is blind imitation of the past...." As such, social prejudices must be overcome if peace is to be established.

The elimination of prejudices is the logical and moral consequence of recognizing the oneness of humanity — that all people are children of God. Social prejudices will be overcome as individuals — particularly children — are educated about the unity of humankind and as this principle is universally proclaimed and applied. According to the Bahá'í teachings, the simple act of informal social interaction with, including offering hospitality to, those of a different race or culture is a powerful and practical means for breaking down prejudices. Overcoming prejudices demands abandoning any subconscious sense of superiority and banishing a patronizing attitude. The goal of conquering prejudices also requires being responsive to the outreach of others, wiping out lingering suspicion, and letting go of the pain of past injustices.

The Equality of Men and Women

At a time in Middle Eastern society when women were considered on the same level as animals and when in the West women lacked the right to vote or own property, Bahá'u'lláh proclaimed the principle of the equality of men and women in rights, privileges, and opportunities. He declared: "Women and men have been and will always be equal in the sight of God." According to the Bahá'í teachings, men and women are as humanity's two wings, and not until both wings are equally developed can the bird of humanity fly. "Woman's lack of progress and proficiency has been due to her need of equal education and opportunity. Had she been allowed this equality, there is no doubt she would be the counterpart of man in ability and capacity."

In the Bahá'í view, the achievement of full equality between men and women is one of the most important prerequisites of peace:

> The denial of such equality perpetrates an injustice against one-half of the world's population and promotes in men harmful attitudes and habits that are carried from the family to the workplace, to political life, and ultimately to international relations.... Only as women are welcomed into full partnership in all fields of human endeavor will the moral and psychological climate be created in which international peace can emerge.

The Bahá'í writings directly link the cessation of war to the achievement of full participation by women in the affairs of the world, including in the arenas of law and politics.

Universal Education

Bahá'u'lláh emphasized the vital role of education in the development of humanity: "Regard man as a mine rich in gems of inestimable value. Education can, alone, cause it to reveal its treasures, and enable mankind to benefit therefrom." The Bahá'í scriptures further state:

> The primary, the most urgent requirement is the promotion of education. It is inconceivable that any nation should achieve prosperity and success unless this paramount, this fundamental concern is carried forward. The principal reason for the decline and fall of peoples is ignorance.

Accordingly, Bahá'u'lláh promoted universal education, with each person receiving training according to his or her capacity. To achieve the goal of universal education, every child must receive education. "If the parents are able to provide the expenses of this education, it is well, otherwise the community must provide the means for the teaching of that child." If resource limitations prevent providing education to everyone in a community, then priority should be given to the education of females:

> Lack of resources limits the ability of many nations to fulfill this necessity, imposing a certain ordering of priorities. The decision-making agencies involved would do well to consider giving first priority to the education of women and girls, since it is through educated mothers that the benefits of knowledge can be most effectively and rapidly diffused throughout society.

Auxiliary International Language

A fundamental barrier to unity and peace is the inability of people from different lands to communicate with one another. In addressing this issue, Bahá'u'lláh advocated the adoption of an auxiliary international language. If an auxiliary language were taught to children in schools worldwide, then over time, people would learn two languages: their native tongue as well as the language used throughout the world. The adoption of an international language "will facilitate intercommunication and dispel the misunderstandings which the barriers of language have occasioned in the world." "Through it sciences and arts will be spread among the nations, and it will prove to be the means of the progress and development of all races." Bahá'u'lláh predicted: "The day is approaching when all the peoples of the world will have adopted one universal language and one common script. When this is achieved, to whatsoever city a man may journey, it shall be as if he were entering his own home."

Economic Justice

Bahá'u'lláh advocated economic justice. From the Bahá'í perspective, a principal cause of economic instability in the world is the great disparity between the rich and the poor. On the one hand, large portions of the world's population lack the most basic material resources, such as clean water, adequate food, or suitable shelter. On the other, there are those whose riches exceed hundreds of millions, and even billions, of dollars. This disparity is contrary to justice. The Bahá'í teachings encourage the adoption of laws — like progressive taxation — that would help eliminate the extremes of wealth and poverty. The goal is not absolute economic equality, which is impossible and undesirable: "absolute equality in fortunes, honors, commerce, agriculture, industry would end in disorderliness, in chaos, in disorganization of the means of existence, and in universal disappointment...." Rather, the goal is a state of balance and moderation in which there will be neither the abnormally rich nor the abject poor.

Moreover, Bahá'u'lláh emphasized the critical role of voluntary sharing in solving economic problems. Addressing the rich, Bahá'u'lláh declared: "The poor in your midst are My trust; guard ye My trust, and be not intent only on your own ease." Because charitable giving is a personally chosen righteous act, the rich should extend assistance to the poor, but of their own free will. Such voluntary giving will lead to greater comfort and economic stability in society.

Universal Peace through Collective Action

Bahá'u'lláh's principle of the oneness of humanity is not merely an expression of vague hope or just a call for a reawakening of the spirit of brotherhood among peoples. Rather, he taught that unity must take form through certain practical steps. Among these are humanity's establishment of an international peace covenant and the exercise of the principle of collective security. Bahá'u'lláh called on the rulers of the nations to come together to deliberate on "such ways and means as will lay the foundations of the world's Great Peace" and to resolve that should any ruler "take up arms against another, all should unitedly arise and prevent him."

The Bahá'í scriptures offer these insights concerning the proceedings for such an international gathering of the world's leaders:

> True civilization will unfurl its banner in the midmost heart of the world whenever a certain number of its distinguished and high-minded sovereigns...

shall, for the good and happiness of all mankind, arise, with firm resolve and clear vision, to establish the Cause of Universal Peace. They must make the Cause of Peace the object of general consultation, and seek by every means in their power to establish a Union of the nations of the world. They must conclude a binding treaty and establish a covenant, the provisions of which shall be sound, inviolable and definite. They must proclaim it to all the world and obtain for it the sanction of all the human race.... In this all-embracing Pact the limits and frontiers of each and every nation should be clearly fixed, the principles underlying the relations of governments towards one another definitely laid down, and all international agreements and obligations ascertained. In like manner, the size of the armaments of every government should be strictly limited, for if the preparations for war and the military forces of any nation should be allowed to increase, they will arouse the suspicion of others. The fundamental principle underlying this solemn Pact should be so fixed that if any government later violate any one of its provisions, all the governments on earth should arise to reduce it to utter submission, nay the human race as a whole should resolve, with every power at its disposal, to destroy that government. Should this greatest of all remedies be applied to the sick body of the world, it will assuredly recover from its ills and will remain eternally safe and secure.

In sum, Bahá'u'lláh affirmed that the "well-being of mankind, its peace and security, are unattainable unless and until its unity is firmly established."

Application of Bahá'í Principles

The peace that Bahá'u'lláh envisioned for the world will emerge as the principles that he identified are increasingly and practically applied. A complete analysis of how Bahá'u'lláh's principles have been, or may be, concretely implemented is beyond the scope of this introduction. However, an example of the practical application of one principle — the equality of men and women — will demonstrate some of the ways in which Bahá'ís have attempted to translate Bahá'u'lláh's lofty teachings into reality.

Bahá'ís have striven to implement the principle of gender equality through education, encouragement, and social and economic development projects. Through his writings and personal conversations, Bahá'u'lláh began a process of educating men and women about the principle of equality. This educational process has since become more formalized and widespread as principles such as gender equality have been taught to Bahá'í children, youth, and adults in classes and conferences worldwide. The Bahá'í community has placed special emphasis on the education of girls. For instance, in the early 1900's, Bahá'ís in Iran, with the assistance of their co-religionists from America, established schools for girls. These schools, which were open to the public, successfully educated many young women throughout the country at a time when such opportunities were practically non-existent for them. By the early 1970's in Iran, literacy rates among Bahá'í women under the age of 40 had reached nearly 100 percent, whereas the national literacy rate for women was less than 25 percent.

This educational process has been complemented by efforts to specifically encourage women to perform important acts of service. For example, in the early 1900's, Bahá'u'lláh's son, who was the head of the Faith at the time, encouraged a woman to spearhead the effort to build the first Bahá'í temple in the West. He asked another Bahá'í woman to organize large-scale, public race unity conferences in the United States. In succeeding years, yet another woman was charged with being the leading representative of the Bahá'í community in meeting with heads of state throughout the world. In these and other ways, Bahá'í women have been encouraged to carry out vital tasks and, in the process, demonstrate their capacity to both genders. Moreover, since the earliest days of the Bahá'í Faith, women have, on their own initiative, arisen to perform heroic acts of service, placing them in the forefront of social change.

Finally, as the human and material resources of the Bahá'í community have grown, efforts have been increasingly made to apply the principle of gender equality through social and economic development projects. For instance, in Africa, Asia, and the Americas, Bahá'ís have initiated development projects to train and empower women in the areas of literacy, hygiene, nutrition, income-generation, and environmental conservation.

While the Bahá'í community has much more work to do in implementing the principle of gender equality, the above approaches have resulted in significant achievements. The substantial number of women actively serving on Bahá'í administrative institutions at local, national, and international levels provides an indication of the success thus far achieved. At the 2008 International Bahá'í Convention, women made up nearly 40% of the elected delegates from more than 150 countries. That such a large percentage of women — many from male-dominated societies — were elected by fellow believers in their home countries shows the degree to which Bahá'í teachings have positively influenced attitudes about the capacity of women to assume responsible positions. Efforts made to apply the principle of gender equality show that Bahá'u'lláh's teachings are not merely theoretical, but are a practical means for promoting unity and peace in the world.

CHAPTER 4

Discovering the Background
of the Bahá'í Teachings:
The History of the Bahá'í Faith

Could such a thing be made manifest
except through the power of
a divine Revelation...?

– BAHÁ'U'LLÁH

The Báb: Manifestation of God and Forerunner

The Bahá'í Faith revolves around three central figures, the first of whom was Mírzá 'Alí-Muhammad, known as the Báb (an Arabic term that is pronounced "Bob" and means "gate"). In May 1844, at the age of 25, the Báb advanced a twofold claim. He declared that he was a Manifestation of God and the forerunner of, or the gate to, one greater than himself who would initiate a new era in the religious history of humanity. The Báb referred to this promised person as "Him Whom God shall make manifest."

The Báb received only an elementary education as a child and began working as a merchant when he was in his teens. Although he had received little formal education, he wrote more than 500,000 verses during his ministry. These writings, which set forth his religious, ethical, and social teachings, challenged the beliefs and social structure of the people of Persia (now Iran). At a time when religious fanaticism was the norm in his country, the Báb taught the ideas of the independent search for the truth, the unity of religion, and the symbolic interpretation of the scriptures. He said humanity was at the beginning of an era that would see the restructuring of all aspects of life. A frequent theme in the Báb's writings was the coming appearance of Him Whom God shall make manifest. Alluding to the station of this anticipated figure, the Báb declared: "Were He to appear this very moment, I would be the first to adore Him, and the first to bow down before Him." The Báb indicated that Him Whom God shall make manifest would appear within nineteen years.

Initially, the Báb attracted to his cause eighteen disciples whom he dispatched throughout Persia and neighboring countries to raise the call that the gate to the Promised One had been opened. After only a few years, thousands of people from all classes of Persian society accepted the Báb's teachings. The growth of his religion alarmed the nation's clergy because they believed and taught that there could be no further revelations from God. Attempting to stop the new religious movement, the clergy enlisted the support of Persian governmental leaders in persecuting the Báb's followers. Such was the Báb's impact that news of him reached the West within a year and a half after he had asserted his claims. An article about the Báb and the persecution of his followers appeared in *The Times* of London in November 1845, and in succeeding months, newspapers in North America and Australia similarly reported about the Báb.

In 1847, as part of their campaign to suppress the Báb's religion, authorities banished him to the remote, northwestern mountains of Persia. Held captive there for nearly three years, the Báb was cut off from his family and his followers and, at times, confined to a solitary cell. When the Báb's isolation and captivity did not produce the desired result, the Persian civil

Opposite: The Shrine of the Báb on the slopes of Mt. Carmel, Haifa, Israel.

and religious authorities began to systematically kill many of the Báb's followers — men, women, and children. Finally, concluding that only the death of the Báb himself could halt the spread of this new religion, Persia's chief governmental officer ordered that the Báb's life be taken. Carrying out this order in July 1850, a firing squad consisting of 750 soldiers executed the Báb in the public square in the city of Tabriz before thousands of onlookers.

In the years immediately preceding and following the Báb's death, nearly 20,000 of his followers were massacred for their religious beliefs. This was in addition to the thousands who were imprisoned, whose homes were pillaged, and whose properties were confiscated. For their refusal to recant their faith, many were put to death after being subjected to horrific torture — their limbs dismembered, their organs gouged out, and their bodies burned. The heroism of the Báb's followers and the cruel manner in which they were killed evoked the sympathy and admiration of a number of Western writers, diplomats, travelers, and scholars, many of whom personally witnessed the appalling scenes. This campaign of persecution nearly destroyed the Báb's religion and took the lives of all of the Báb's eminent supporters except one.

Bahá'u'lláh: Promoter of the Báb's Religion and Manifestation of God

The only prominent disciple of the Báb who survived the campaign of persecution was Mírzá Husayn-'Alí, better known as Bahá'u'lláh (an Arabic term meaning "the Glory of God"). Bahá'u'lláh was born in 1817 into a wealthy family. His father was a provincial minister in the Persian government. Upon the passing of his father, Bahá'u'lláh was invited to take his father's high governmental position, but he declined the offer of worldly power. Instead, he chose to focus on activities that served the poor and the oppressed. By the early 1840's, Baháʾuʾlláh's philanthropy and generosity had become so widely recognized that he was called the "Father of the Poor."

Soon after the Báb declared his mission in 1844, he directed his first disciple to travel to the capital and deliver to Baháʾuʾlláh some of the Báb's writings. Upon reviewing these writings, Baháʾuʾlláh immediately accepted the truth of the Báb's claim. In the following years, Baháʾuʾlláh played a significant role in spreading the Báb's religion and guiding its development. Through correspondence, Baháʾuʾlláh maintained close contact with the Báb. Shortly before his death, the Báb directed that his documents and important possessions be delivered to Baháʾuʾlláh.

Because of the important role he had played in promoting the Báb's message, Baháʾuʾlláh was arrested and imprisoned in 1852. He and other followers of the Báb were confined in the Persian capital's underground dungeon infamously known as "the Black Pit." This was a stench-filled, vermin-infested jail that usually housed murderers, thieves, and other criminals. During his four-month imprisonment in the Black Pit, Baháʾuʾlláh's feet were placed in stocks, his hands were cuffed behind his back, and his neck was weighed down by chains exceeding 110 pounds (51 kg). While in this condition, Baháʾuʾlláh's mission as a Manifestation of God was born. He later described how he became aware of the mission God conferred upon him:

> I was but a man like others, asleep upon My couch, when lo, the breezes of the All-Glorious were wafted over Me, and taught Me the knowledge of all that hath been. This thing is not from Me, but from One Who is Almighty and All-Knowing. And He bade Me lift up My voice between earth and heaven, and for this there befell Me what hath

caused the tears of every man of understanding to flow. The learning current amongst men I studied not; their schools I entered not.… The hand of the will of thy Lord, the Compassionate, the Merciful, transformed Me.

The Exiles of Bahá'u'lláh

Bahá'u'lláh was eventually released from prison, but immediately ordered to leave the country. As a result, in 1853, Bahá'u'lláh and some members of his family left Persia for Baghdad, Iraq. In Baghdad, which was then part of the Turkish empire, Bahá'u'lláh set about to revive what remained of the persecuted community of the Báb's followers. Through his teaching and writing, he was able to unify and strengthen the community. He also earned the respect of scholars, mystics,

Map illustrating Bahá'u'lláh's successive exiles.

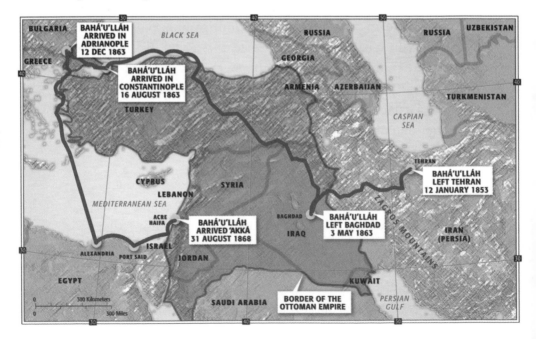

and government officials, including the governor of Baghdad and the British counsel-general. While in Baghdad, Bahá'u'lláh wrote the *Book of Certitude*, wherein he addressed the long-standing barriers that have separated the followers of different religions and explained how those barriers can be overcome. He also penned the *Hidden Words*, a collection of short utterances that present the essence of past religious teachings.

In 1863 — nineteen years after the inception of the Báb's Faith — Bahá'u'lláh declared to his companions that he was the Manifestation of God whom the Báb had anticipated. As his declaration became known among the Báb's followers, the vast majority accepted Bahá'u'lláh's claim.

The Persian government had expected Bahá'u'lláh's banishment to a foreign country to stifle the growth of the cause he was promoting. But when it became clear that Bahá'u'lláh was attracting the attention and admiration of influential persons in Baghdad and beyond, Persian authorities pressured Turkish officials to exile Bahá'u'lláh farther away from Persia. As a result, in 1863, the Sultan of Turkey ordered the transfer of Bahá'u'lláh to Constantinople (now Istanbul) and a few months later to Adrianople (now Edirne) in the western extremity of the empire. Bahá'u'lláh and his fellow exiles lived in Adrianople from late 1863 until 1868.

In Adrianople, Bahá'u'lláh again earned the admiration of prominent individuals. At the same time, his religion continued to spread in Persia. Urged on by Persian authorities, Turkish officials finally determined they would isolate Bahá'u'lláh by imprisoning him in the notorious prison-city of 'Akká, Palestine (now Israel). Filthy, disease-ridden, of foul climate, lacking vegetation, and without any source of water within its gates, 'Akká was a place reserved for dangerous criminals and political prisoners from throughout the Turkish empire. Though they had committed no crime, Bahá'u'lláh, his family, and a company of his followers (which included men, women, and children) were banished there in 1868. Such were the conditions in 'Akká that shortly after their arrival, three of the exiles died from illness and nearly all of the others fell ill to malaria, dysentery, and other diseases.

The rigorous imprisonment of Bahá'u'lláh and his companions lasted two years. As the local authorities became acquainted with Bahá'u'lláh's noble character and teachings, they gradually relaxed the harsh and restrictive prison conditions. Though his confinement order was never formally lifted, Bahá'u'lláh was eventually able to leave the prison-city. Over time, local officials began paying their respects to him and seeking his advice.

Bahá'u'lláh spent the last 24 years of his life in and near 'Akká. His successive banishments had the effect of involuntarily transferring him to the Holy Land — the land considered sacred by the followers of Judaism, Christianity, and Islam.

The Writings of Bahá'u'lláh

During his exile, Bahá'u'lláh wrote the equivalent of 100 volumes — one of the largest bodies of religious writing ever produced by an individual. In these writings, he expounded his religion's spiritual and social principles, set forth its laws, and established institutions to safeguard its integrity and unity. Among Bahá'u'lláh's writings are his epistles to the most powerful political and religious rulers of the time — Napoleon III of France, the Czar of Russia, the Sultan of Turkey, the Shah of Persia, Pope Pius IX, Muslim clergymen, and others. In these writings, Bahá'u'lláh announced the advent of the day of God, set forth his claim, admonished the rulers to uphold the principles of justice and unity, exhorted them to reduce their armaments, and advised them to establish peace through international agreement and collective security. Moreover, he counseled them to end the excessive financial burdens impoverishing their subjects, warned them of the consequences of their rejection of his message, and denounced, in some cases, their arrogance and tyranny.

For example, to Napoleon III, Bahá'u'lláh addressed an epistle wherein he prophesied Napoleon's downfall: "thy kingdom shall be thrown into confusion, and thine empire shall pass from thine hands...." Not long after this epistle was published and disseminated, Napoleon III suffered a humiliating defeat in 1870 at the battle of Sedan that led to the loss of his empire. Similar predictions appeared in Bahá'u'lláh's epistles to other rulers. The dramatic fulfillment of Bahá'u'lláh's widely-circulated prophecies added to his prestige.

That a prisoner — captive in a foreign country and without a defender — would with such authority address those who held the power of death over him presents one of the most remarkable episodes in religious history. Even more striking is the contrast between the downfall of the kings and rulers whom Bahá'u'lláh addressed and whose fate he accurately predicted, and the ascent of the movement he espoused, which, within less than a century of his passing, would spread to nearly every country around the globe.

The Sufferings of Bahá'u'lláh

In 1892, Bahá'u'lláh passed away near 'Akká, where his shrine is located today. His death was mourned by his own followers, as well as by governmental leaders, intellectuals, and notables from the Jewish, Christian, and Muslim communities in the Holy Land. Thus ended a life that had endured nearly a half-century of suffering. While in his mid-30's, Bahá'u'lláh had been imprisoned for four months among criminals of the worst order in a dark and filthy underground dungeon, and on his neck had been placed such heavy chains that the marks of this torture remained on his body for the rest of his life.

The Shrine of Bahá'u'lláh near 'Akká, Israel.

Bahá'u'lláh's wealth and property had been confiscated. Later, he had been forced out of his native land. Though he had committed no crime, he was compelled to live 40 years as a prisoner and an exile and to endure four successive banishments. During his exile, attempts were made on his life, including two occasions when he was poisoned, the latter occasion causing an extended illness and leaving him with a permanent tremor. Finally, he had been incarcerated in the desolate and disease-infested city of 'Akká. It was within the prison of 'Akká where one of Bahá'u'lláh's sons died before his eyes.

Why did Bahá'u'lláh submit to such sufferings? Why would one who had been reared in the lap of luxury and wealth and who had a prominent governmental position awaiting him choose a path that would lead to such pain and deprivation? Why did he not abandon his beliefs when doing so would have stopped his persecution and allowed him and his family to pursue a life of comfort? Insights into these questions are found in Bahá'u'lláh's own writings. Referring to himself while imprisoned, he wrote:

> The Ancient Beauty [Bahá'u'lláh] hath consented to be bound with chains that mankind may be released from its bondage, and hath accepted to be made a prisoner within this most mighty Stronghold that the whole world may attain unto true liberty. He hath drained to its dregs the cup of sorrow, that all the peoples of the earth may attain unto abiding joy, and be filled with gladness.

Bahá'u'lláh further declared: "We have accepted to be abased...that ye may be exalted, and have suffered manifold afflictions, that ye might prosper and flourish." Bahá'u'lláh "bore these ordeals, suffered these calamities and difficulties in order that a manifestation of selflessness and service might become apparent in the world of humanity" and that through the promotion of his teachings, human beings would develop their spiritual capacities and establish a society that functioned according to the principles of justice and unity. In sum, it was because of his love for humanity and his desire for the betterment of the world that Bahá'u'lláh endured hardships and ordeals and sacrificed for nearly a half century.

'Abdu'l-Bahá: Successor and Interpreter

To ensure that his religion would maintain its integrity and unity and not become divided or dissipated upon his death, Bahá'u'lláh explicitly identified his successor and created an administrative order that would guide his Faith for centuries into the future. In his writings, Bahá'u'lláh designated as his immediate successor his eldest son, Abbas Effendi, who, after the passing of his father, adopted the name 'Abdu'l-Bahá (pro-nounced "Ab-Dol-Ba-Ha," this Arabic term means "Servant of Bahá"). Bahá'u'lláh declared that 'Abdu'l-Bahá was the autho-rized interpreter of the Bahá'í teachings and the center to whom all Bahá'ís should turn for instruction and guidance. As the third of the Bahá'í Faith's three central figures, 'Abdu'l-Bahá carried out these functions from the time of Bahá'u'lláh's passing until his own death three decades later.

Born in 1844, 'Abdu'l-Bahá shared his father's suc-cessive banishments and imprisonment. 'Abdu'l-Bahá offi-cially remained a prisoner until 1908, when a revolution in the Turkish empire resulted in the release of all religious and political prisoners. Shortly after he was freed, and despite his advanced age and poor health caused by nearly a half-cen-tury of exile and confinement, he embarked upon a three-year teaching tour through Egypt, Europe, and North America.

Lacking any formal schooling, unfamiliar with Western customs and languages, and having never previously faced a public audience, 'Abdu'l-Bahá arose to proclaim Bahá'u'lláh's teachings in churches, synagogues, universities, and other pub-lic forums before audiences that, at times, exceeded a thousand people. In addition to conducting numerous private interviews and informal discussions, he delivered in nearly 40 cities of the United States and Canada some 140 talks, which were trans-lated into English for his audiences. He spoke at Columbia, Howard, and New York Universities; lectured before 1,800 stu-dents and 180 teachers at Stanford University; and addressed the fourth annual conference of the National Association for the Advancement of Colored People (NAACP). Secretaries of state, ambassadors, congressmen, distinguished rabbis and church leaders, university presidents, and other eminent individuals, including Theodore Roosevelt, Alexander Graham Bell, Andrew Carnegie, and Admiral Robert Peary, were among those who visited 'Abdu'l-Bahá during his stay in America in 1912.

'Abdu'l-Bahá on his 1912 visit to the United States.

Beyond proclaiming Bahá'u'lláh's teachings in words, 'Abdu'l-Bahá demonstrated them in deeds. For example, the depth of 'Abdu'l-Bahá's love for humanity and his forgiveness of his enemies were exemplified when in France he encountered an exiled Persian prince. This prince had been the cause of much suffering for the Bahá'í community, as he had, during his governorship, ratified the killing of prominent Bahá'ís. Upon meeting 'Abdu'l-Bahá, the prince attempted to offer excuses for his past conduct. 'Abdu'l-Bahá's response was: "All that is of the past. Never think of it again."

Moreover, 'Abdu'l-Bahá's courageous commitment to unity was clear during an era of racial segregation in America. For example, at a formal luncheon held in his honor in Washington, D.C., he insisted that a black American friend be allowed to attend and be given the seat of honor. 'Abdu'l-Bahá then proceeded to deliver a talk on the theme of the unity of mankind.

During his travels, 'Abdu'l-Bahá refused any compensation for his lectures and chose the most modest accommodations and travel arrangements for himself, yet he gave generously to the poor and needy wherever he went. At all times, he strove to be of service to others, emphasizing that service to humanity is service to God. Because of 'Abdu'l-Bahá's humanitarian work during the first World War in relieving famine and distress, British authorities conferred the honor of knighthood upon him in 1920.

'Abdu'l-Bahá's legacy was broad and lasting. As a result of his efforts, the Bahá'í Faith became firmly established in North America and Europe. Through his encouragement, it was also carried to Australia and the Far East. At his urging, Persian Bahá'ís established schools — open to people of all faiths — at a time when an educational system in Iran was practically non-existent. And under his guidance, Bahá'ís developed administrative councils, often in cultures unfamiliar with group decision-making. Finally, he left for posterity dozens of volumes of writings that interpreted, expounded on, and applied Bahá'u'lláh's teachings.

Through his words and example, 'Abdu'l-Bahá helped unify people of various nationalities, races, and religions. When 'Abdu'l-Bahá passed away in 1921, his funeral was a testimony to what he had achieved, as no fewer than ten thousand people of every class, race, and religion in the Holy Land — including the Governors of Jerusalem and Phoenicia and dignitaries of the Jewish, Christian, and Muslim communities — paid tribute to his accomplishments in promoting unity, peace, and service to humanity.

The Bahá'í Administrative Order

After his passing, 'Abdu'l-Bahá's role in leading the Bahá'í Faith was succeeded by the Bahá'í administrative order, whose institutions and principles Bahá'u'lláh and 'Abdu'l-Bahá had set forth in their writings. Specifically, they had ordained the institutions of the Guardian and of the Universal House of Justice as the two pillars of the Bahá'í administrative order, invested these institutions with the authority to preserve the integrity and unity of the Bahá'í Faith, and assured both of divine guidance. According to the Bahá'í scriptures, the Guardian was the authorized interpreter of the Bahá'í teachings, and the Universal House of Justice was invested with the function of legislating on matters not expressly revealed in the Bahá'í writings. Bahá'u'lláh and 'Abdu'l-Bahá empowered both institutions to apply the Faith's principles, promulgate its laws, and adapt its teachings to meet the needs of an evolving society.

In his Will and Testament, 'Abdu'l-Bahá designated his eldest grandson, Shoghi Effendi, as Guardian of the Bahá'í Faith. Shoghi Effendi assumed this office upon 'Abdu'l-Bahá's passing and began the process of building up the local and national institutions, called Spiritual Assemblies, that would support the Universal House of Justice, an internationally elected council. Through his writings, Shoghi Effendi educated Bahá'ís in how Spiritual Assemblies were to be elected — democratically through secret-ballot elections devoid of nominations or campaigning. He also emphasized that Bahá'í institutions must use the decision-making process of consultation, which is governed by spiritual principles. By his passing in 1957, Shoghi Effendi had led the worldwide Bahá'í community in establishing hundreds of local Spiritual Assemblies around the globe and had raised up national Spiritual Assemblies in 26 countries. The vast expansion of the Bahá'í community resulted from systematic teaching plans that Shoghi Effendi had encouraged Bahá'ís to carry out. Because the religion lacks clergy or professional missionaries, the Bahá'í teachings spread as individual Bahá'ís traveled or relocated to new areas.

Shoghi Effendi also developed the international center of the Bahá'í Faith in 'Akká and Haifa, Israel. Finally, he deepened

believers' understanding of the Bahá'í teachings through his interpretations, contained in his numerous letters, which number in the tens of thousands. His writings are a source of continuing guidance for Bahá'ís.

After Shoghi Effendi's passing, the Faith was led for six years by a group of eminent believers whom he had designated for the purposes of protecting and spreading the Faith. In 1963, upon the completion of a ten-year plan Shoghi Effendi had launched a decade earlier, members of national Spiritual Assemblies from around the world elected the Universal House of Justice. Like other Bahá'í elections, the election of the nine members of the House of Justice was carried out by secret-ballot vote without nominations or electioneering. Since that first election, the members of the House of Justice have been elected in the same manner every five years. At the 2008 election, more than 1,000 men and women, representing Bahá'í communities in 166 nations, cast their votes in the election of the House of Justice. With its seat on Mt. Carmel in Israel, in the shadow of the shrines of the Báb and of Bahá'u'lláh, the House of Justice has been, since its formation, the Faith's supreme institution to which all the Bahá'ís of the world turn.

Like the Guardian before it, the House of Justice has coordinated and directed the work of the worldwide Bahá'í community and led it in spreading the Bahá'í Faith's teachings, consolidating its communities, and promoting the spiritual education of children, youth, and adults. The House of Justice has also guided believers in applying the Bahá'í teachings — for example, in the fields of social and economic development — in ways that will improve the lives of people and address the concrete challenges facing humanity. Moreover, it has encouraged the Bahá'í community to work

Opposite: The Seat of the Universal House of Justice, in Haifa, Israel.

with like-minded organizations in promoting peace and development. For decades, the Bahá'í international community has been accredited as a non-governmental organization at the United Nations and has held consultative status with the Economic and Social Council and various specialized agencies.

Finally, like 'Abdu'l-Bahá and Shoghi Effendi, the Universal House of Justice has preserved the integrity of the Bahá'í teachings and maintained the unity of the Bahá'í Faith.

CHAPTER 5

Adopting Spiritual Patterns:
Laws and Principles for the Individual, the Family, and the Community

*Observe ye the statutes and precepts of
your Lord, and walk ye in this Way
which hath been laid out before you....*

– BAHÁ'U'LLÁH

The Purposes of Divine Laws and Principles

In his writings, Bahá'u'lláh set forth laws and principles for the individual, the family, and the community. These ordinances are not a mere code of laws — arbitrary dos and don'ts. Rather, they are spiritual patterns through which humanity may attain happiness: "Happy are they that observe God's precepts...." Moreover, as Bahá'u'lláh has declared, his laws provide the key to freedom: "True liberty consisteth in man's submission unto My commandments...."

Why does observance of divine ordinances result in happiness and freedom? As the Bahá'í scriptures explain, "human happiness is founded upon spiritual behavior." Bahá'u'lláh's laws and principles spiritualize the life of the individual, increase understanding, and raise the standard of behavior. As the individual strives to behave in accord with these spiritual patterns, transformative forces operate upon his or her soul. The outcome of such obedience to God's laws and principles is acquisition of spiritual and moral character. Conforming to divine patterns also strengthens marriage and family life and promotes the unity of communities. Adherence to these spiritual standards allows individuals, families, and communities to be liberated from selfishness, hatred, conflict, and oppression and to be free to progress spiritually and materially. Just as appreciating nature's laws enables one to live in harmony with the forces of the physical world, observance of God's laws and teachings frees us from untold spiritual and moral difficulties.

Observing God's teachings attracts benefits and blessings. But, according to the Bahá'í view, the motivation to carry out divine laws and principles should not be merely the hope for reward or fear of punishment. Ideally, one should strive to obey God's teachings to express one's love for God. Bahá'u'lláh counseled: "Observe ye the commandments of God for love of His beauty...."

Below is a discussion of some important Bahá'í laws and principles applicable to the individual, the family, and the community.

The Individual

Laws and principles for the individual may be summarized as follows:

- Daily prayer and meditation
- Regular study of the sacred scriptures
- Service to others
- Sharing God's teachings with others
- Material offerings
- Various provisions related to personal conduct

Prayer is among the most important spiritual laws prescribed for the individual. According to the Bahá'í teachings, prayer is conversation with God and the chief means to cultivate spirituality. Prayer strengthens, revives, and purifies the soul and, thus, insures its development. Just as the physical body needs to be fed every day, the soul also needs the daily nourishment of prayer to grow spiritually.

In the Bahá'í Faith, prayer takes two forms: daily Obligatory Prayers and other prayers. Bahá'u'lláh decreed that each believer should recite daily one of three Obligatory Prayers according to certain prescribed requirements. For example, the individual may offer the Short Obligatory Prayer — set forth below — by reciting it once a day between noon and sunset:

> I bear witness, O my God, that Thou hast created me to know Thee and to worship Thee. I testify, at this moment, to my powerlessness and to Thy might, to my poverty and to Thy wealth.
>
> There is none other God but Thee, the Help in Peril, the Self-Subsisting.

In addition to offering a daily Obligatory Prayer, the individual is encouraged to pray on other occasions. Bahá'u'lláh, the Báb, and 'Abdu'l-Bahá have revealed many prayers on themes such as assistance, children, families, healing, overcoming difficulties, and spiritual growth. Prayer can also be purely spontaneous and recited in one's own words.

Prayer is complemented by the spiritual practice of meditation. Whereas prayer is conversation with God, meditation is conversation with one's own soul: "In that state of mind you put certain questions to your spirit and the spirit answers: the light breaks forth and the reality is revealed." "Through meditation the doors of deeper knowledge and inspiration may be opened." As the Bahá'í writings further explain,

> It is not sufficient to pray diligently for guidance, but this prayer must be followed by meditation as to the best methods of action and then action itself. Even if the action should not immediately produce

results, or perhaps not be entirely correct, that does not make so much difference, because prayers can only be answered through action and if someone's action is wrong, God can use that method of showing the pathway which is right.

There is no set technique of meditation prescribed in the Bahá'í teachings, so the manner of doing so is left to the individual.

Regular study of the sacred scriptures is another law ordained for the individual. Bahá'u'lláh wrote: "Immerse yourselves in the ocean of My words, that ye may unravel its secrets, and discover all the pearls of wisdom that lie hid in its depths." Because of the absence of clergy in the Bahá'í Faith and because of the principle of independent investigation of the truth, every believer has the sacred obligation to individually study the Bahá'í writings: "the Teachings of Bahá'u'lláh should be carefully studied, one by one, until they are realized and understood by mind and heart...." The understanding of the Word of God is not dependent upon human learning, but is conditioned upon "purity of heart, chastity of soul, and freedom of spirit."

Serving others is yet another spiritual principle for the individual: "Service to humanity is service to God." One form of service is engaging in an occupation. Under Bahá'í law, every person should be occupied in a profession, trade, craft, or work (which includes homemaking). Engagement in an occupation, when prompted by the highest motives and the desire to be of service to humanity, constitutes worship of God. In addition to pursuing an occupation, individuals are encouraged to render service to others in their daily interactions: "Think ye at all times of rendering some service to every member of the human race." One should strive to do some good to every person whose path he or she crosses.

Another sacred obligation for Bahá'ís is sharing God's teachings with others. Bahá'u'lláh prohibited his followers from spreading his Faith by violence, force, or coercion. Rather, the Word of God should be shared with respect and love, as if offering a gift to a friend. Bahá'u'lláh explained:

> The children of men are all brothers, and the prerequisites of brotherhood are manifold. Among them is that one should wish for one's brother that which one wisheth for oneself. Therefore, it behoveth him who is the recipient of an inward or outward gift or who partaketh of the bread of heaven to inform and invite his friends with the utmost love and kindness. If they respond favourably, his object is attained; otherwise he should leave them to themselves without contending with them or uttering a word that would cause the least sadness.

Yet another spiritual obligation for individual Bahá'ís is making material offerings for their Faith. The privilege of making these offerings is reserved for Bahá'ís only; the Bahá'í Faith does not solicit or accept offerings from those who are not Bahá'ís. Material offerings take two forms. The first is a law called "the Right of God" under which individuals — after providing for their own essential expenses — pay a fixed portion of the remaining value of their assets to the head of the Faith (the Universal House of Justice). The second is the practice of contributing to the Bahá'í Fund. "Contributing to the Fund is a service that every believer can render, be he poor or wealthy...." Funds may be contributed at the local, national, and international levels. With regard to both the Right of God and the Fund, the Bahá'í sacred writings emphasize the importance of the principle of dignity. Bahá'u'lláh warned: "It would be impossible to conceive any act more contemptible than soliciting, in the name of the one true God, the riches which men possess." As such, within the Bahá'í community, no believer may be approached individually to pay the Right of God or to contribute to the Fund. Moreover, whether or how much one has offered is not public information. Rather, the confidentiality of material offerings is strictly maintained by the Bahá'í institution receiving them.

In addition to the above spiritual practices, the Bahá'í scriptures set forth other laws. Among the most vital is the practice of fasting. Bahá'u'lláh enjoined his followers to fast from sunrise to sunset each day during the period March 2nd through March 20th (the last month of the year in the Bahá'í calendar). The purpose of the fast is fundamentally spiritual: a symbol and reminder of abstinence from selfish and bodily desires. The fast is binding on those between the ages of 15 and 70. Bahá'ís who are ill, traveling, pregnant, or nursing are exempt from fasting.

Other Bahá'í laws applicable to the individual include a prohibition on gossip and backbiting — the practice of discussing the faults of others in their absence. The Bahá'í scriptures identify backbiting as the worst human quality because it hampers the spiritual growth of the individual and undermines the unity of the community. Bahá'u'lláh wrote that "backbiting quencheth the light of the heart, and extinguisheth the life of the soul." He further counseled: "Breathe not the sins of others so long as thou art thyself a sinner," and "magnify not the faults of others that thine own faults may not appear great." 'Abdu'l-Bahá offered this advice on avoiding backbiting:

> Whenever you recognize the fault of another, think of yourself! What are my imperfections? — and try to remove them. Do this whenever you are tried through the words or deeds of others. Thus you will grow, become more perfect. You will overcome self, you will not even have time to think of the faults of others....

Bahá'u'lláh prohibited his followers from consuming alcohol or using mind-altering drugs (such as marijuana, opium, LSD, and other hallucinogenic substances) unless prescribed by a qualified physician as part of a medical treatment. The negative social consequences of the use of alcohol and narcotics are severe. Every year, alcohol and illicit drug use account for nearly two million deaths worldwide; result in an even greater number of injuries; cause significant birth defects; contribute to domestic violence and family breakdown; and impose staggering economic costs in health care and lost productivity. Moreover, consumption of alcohol and narcotics temporarily (and sometimes permanently) inhibits the proper functioning of the human mind — the essential quality of the soul. Therefore, their use does not befit the noble station with which God has endowed human beings: "Noble have I created thee, yet thou hast abased thyself. Rise then unto that for which thou wast created." Bahá'u'lláh wrote: "It is inadmissible that man, who hath been endowed with reason, should consume that which stealeth it away." Among other laws and principles applicable to the individual are being chaste before marriage and faithful during marriage.

Further, while loyal to the government and free to vote in elections, Bahá'ís do not take part in partisan politics, for example, by running for office or being members of political parties. Membership in a political party would necessarily entail repudiating at least some Bahá'í principles as there is no party whose principles are fully aligned with the Bahá'í teachings. If Bahá'ís participated in partisan politics and chose to join different parties, they would be working against one another, which would be inconsistent with the Bahá'í goal of promoting unity.

Beyond setting out the laws and principles that will allow the individual to grow spiritually, Bahá'u'lláh also offered guidance on the role of tests and difficulties in the soul's spiritual development. According to the Bahá'í teachings, the trials that people face are of two kinds. First, there are difficulties that are the consequences of one's poor choices. For example, if a person poisons his body by taking illicit drugs or gambles away his savings, the sorrows are caused by his own unwise actions. Second, there are trials that are divinely-intended to develop the individual's spiritual potential. As 'Abdu'l-Bahá explained:

> The mind and spirit of man advance when he is tried by suffering. The more the ground is ploughed the better the seed will grow, the better the harvest will be. Just as the plough furrows the earth deeply, purifying it of weeds and thistles, so suffering and tribulation free man from the petty affairs of this worldly life until he arrives at a state of complete detachment.

Tests and difficulties teach the individual to rely upon God. Importantly, while some trials may seem unbearable, Bahá'u'lláh gave the assurance that no one will be tested beyond his or her capacity: "God hath never burdened any soul beyond its power." The soul that steadfastly obeys the Manifestation's teachings and follows spiritual principle in the face of difficulties will grow spiritually.

As individuals carry out Bahá'u'lláh's laws and principles, they will gradually come to see in themselves the benefits conferred by these ordinances.

The Family

The Bahá'í teachings encourage marriage, describing it as a sacred institution that can be a source of well-being, happiness, and security. In marriage, the husband and wife should be united physically and spiritually that they may ever improve each other's spiritual life. While the physical aspect of marriage must be given its due importance, it is subordinate to the moral and spiritual purposes and functions of the institution. Of primary importance is that husband and wife should live their lives in love and harmony. If they are unified, "they will pass through this world with perfect contentment, bliss, and peace of heart, and become the object of divine grace and favor in the Kingdom of heaven."

One of the keys to strengthening the unity between husband and wife is loving consultation — a practice prescribed by Bahá'u'lláh to assist married couples, communities, institutions, or any group of people seeking to solve problems. As summarized below, the process of consultation set out in the Bahá'í scriptures is not merely group discussion or the voicing of personal opinions. Instead, it is a decision-making process based on spiritual principles, qualities, and actions.

The first condition of consultation is absolute love and harmony among those consulting. The second condition is that participants seek God's assistance through prayer. After fulfilling these conditions, the couple (or group) must search out the truth. Participants must, with complete freedom, express their own thoughts on the question before them, but they must not belittle the thoughts of others. They must communicate with courtesy, dignity, care, and moderation. The spark of truth appears when differing opinions clash. Moreover,

> He who expresses an opinion should not voice it as correct and right but set it forth as a contribution to the consensus of opinion…. If he finds that a previously expressed opinion is more true and worthy, he should accept it immediately and not willfully hold to an opinion of his own. By this excellent method he endeavors to arrive at unity and truth.

By contrast, "stubbornness and persistence in one's views will lead ultimately to discord and wrangling and the truth will remain hidden."

In any group, however loving the consultation, there may be times when agreement cannot be reached. When the group consists of three or more people, this dilemma is resolved by majority vote. Obviously, there can be no majority where only two people are consulting, as with a husband and wife. Therefore, there are times "when a wife should defer to her husband, and times when a husband should defer to his wife, but neither should ever unjustly dominate the other." It is for each couple to determine under what circumstances such deference should take place.

Once a couple or a group reaches a decision in consultation, then all must wholeheartedly support the outcome, even if one personally disagrees with the decision. "If they agree upon a subject, even though it be wrong, it is better than to disagree and be in the right, for this difference will produce the demolition of the divine foundation.… [B]ut if they agree and both parties are in the wrong, as it is in unity the truth will be revealed and the wrong made right." By unitedly putting into action and supporting the decision arrived at during consultation, the couple or group can determine whether, in fact, the correct decision has been reached. If it becomes clear that the initial decision was not correct or effective, then the couple or group consults again, arriving at and supporting another decision together. By maintaining unity through consultation, the best solution will eventually be discovered. From the Bahá'í perspective, family consultation "employing full and frank discussion, and animated by awareness of the need for moderation and balance, can be the panacea for domestic conflict."

Unity between husband and wife provides the ideal environment for the rearing and spiritual training of children. The Bahá'í scriptures call on the father and mother to make every effort to train their children spiritually (in morals and good conduct) and intellectually (in reading, writing, the sciences, and the arts). Approximately a century ago, 'Abdu'l-Bahá made this prediction about the future condition of the world and the importance of the education of children:

> In a time to come, morals will degenerate to an extreme degree. It is essential that children be reared in the Bahá'í way, that they may find happiness both in this world and the next. If not, they shall be beset by sorrows and troubles, for human happiness is founded upon spiritual behavior.

He further emphasized that the highest priority should be given to moral training:

> Training in morals and good conduct is far more important than book learning. A child that is cleanly, agreeable, of good character, well-behaved — even though he be ignorant — is preferable to a child that is rude, unwashed, ill-natured, and yet becoming deeply versed in all the sciences and arts. The reason for this is that the child who conducts himself well, even though he be ignorant, is of benefit to others, while an ill-natured, ill-behaved child is corrupted and harmful to others, even though he be learned. If, however, the child be trained to be both learned and good, the result is light upon light.

The Bahá'í scriptures offer many insights on the subject of the education of children. Among them is that it is much easier to morally train children when they are young: "children, at the beginning of life, are fresh and tender as a young twig, and can be trained in any fashion you desire." But moral education becomes more challenging once children pass the age of puberty. Moreover, while parents are enjoined to educate all of their children, the Bahá'í teachings specify that if resources are limited, then preference should be given to the education of girls: the training of daughters is essential because "it is through educated mothers that the benefits of knowledge can be most effectively and rapidly diffused throughout society."

In molding their children's moral character, parents are encouraged to apply the principle of unity at all times: the "integrity of the family bond must be constantly considered, and the rights of the individual members must not be transgressed.... The injury of one shall be considered the injury of all; the comfort of each, the comfort of all; the honor of one, the honor of all." "If love and agreement are manifest in a single family, that family will advance, become illumined and spiritual; but if enmity and hatred exist within it, destruction and dispersion are inevitable."

The Community

The Bahá'í teachings also address the development of community life. The active participation of the individual in the devotional, educational, social, and administrative activities of the Bahá'í community fosters spiritual growth because it deepens his or her understanding of the tenets of the Bahá'í Faith and provides a laboratory for translating them into action. Through such participation, each person is able to contribute to building a spiritual civilization. There are four core activities that Bahá'í community life promotes: devotional gatherings, study circles, children's classes, and groups for the moral empowerment of young teenagers. All of these activities are open to the public.

The Bahá'í scriptures encourage the holding of regular devotional gatherings, meetings where individuals come together to "glorify God and fix their hearts upon Him, and read and recite the holy writings." Such gatherings — which may be held in homes, in Bahá'í centers where available, or elsewhere — are essential to the spiritual life of the community.

At devotional gatherings, Bahá'ís are encouraged to use the prayers and writings of Bahá'u'lláh, the Báb, and 'Abdu'l-Bahá and may also include the sacred scriptures of other religions. Music, which is considered a ladder for the soul, may be incorporated during devotional gatherings. No set form is prescribed for such gatherings. They may have different formats depending on the tastes and cultural backgrounds of the participants.

'Abdu'l-Bahá also encouraged the holding of meetings for the study of the Bahá'í teachings, history, and proofs. Bahá'ís and their friends come together in small groups called study circles to systematically explore the meaning and application of Bahá'u'lláh's teachings. In the Bahá'í view, understanding increases when study and service are joined and carried out together. Study circles, which are participatory in format and facilitated by fellow community members, allow individuals to combine these elements of study and service.

Children's classes are a third core activity of the Bahá'í community. According to the Bahá'í scriptures, among "the greatest of all services that can possibly be rendered by man to Almighty God is the education and training of children...." Bahá'í children's classes attempt to nurture the spiritual capacities of the youngest members of the community and help them develop noble and upright characters. In addition, moral empowerment groups for young teenagers encourage the development of spiritual identity through study, service, and the arts.

Because these core activities provide spiritual nourishment and education, they are viewed by Bahá'ís as essential to developing a unified and nurturing community environment. Instead of having a few centralized activities for an entire town or city, Bahá'ís are encouraged to take initiative at the neighborhood level in order that more people may have the opportunity to take part in the core activities and so that a sense of community emerges locally. Bahá'ís invite their friends,

Core activities in Bahá'í communities: devotional gatherings, study circles, children's classes, and groups for young teenagers.

neighbors, and co-workers to participate in, and contribute their energies and talents in promoting, these core elements of community life.

As local Bahá'í communities grow and are able to sustain the above core activities, they have the opportunity to further develop by introducing projects concerned with social and economic development. Depending on their size and resources, communities may undertake simple (and, over time, more sophisticated) projects in the fields of agriculture, education, environmental preservation, health, literacy, rural development, race unity, or others. In addition to some 600 ongoing, socio-economic development projects, Bahá'ís worldwide are currently supporting several thousand smaller projects of fixed duration. Regardless of their size, such projects are a means for applying spiritual principles to the practical life of humanity and for promoting spiritual and material prosperity.

Another vital community activity for Bahá'ís is the Nineteen Day Feast — a regular gathering that focuses on the spiritual, administrative, and social aspects of Bahá'í community life. The institution of the Feast has a devotional part during which prayers and sacred scriptures are recited. This is followed by an administrative segment during which the local Spiritual Assembly (the Bahá'í community's local governing council) reports its plans and activities, shares news and messages, and receives the thoughts and recommendations of community members through the process of consultation. The Feast, thus, provides an arena of democracy that connects the local community with the whole of the worldwide Bahá'í administrative order. The third part of the Feast — the social portion — involves the partaking of refreshments and engaging in other activities meant to foster fellowship in the community.

As its name indicates, the Nineteen Day Feast is held once every nineteen days, at the beginning of each Bahá'í month. (The Bahá'í calendar has nineteen months, each of which has nineteen days.) "Attendance at Nineteen Day Feasts is not obligatory but very important, and every believer should consider it a duty and privilege to be present on such occasions." Unlike the core activities of the Bahá'í community, which are all open to the public, attendance at Feast is limited to Bahá'ís because of its administrative element. In addition to the Feast, each year, Bahá'ís observe nine holy days, most of which are associated with significant events in the lives of the Faith's three central figures. On these holy days — during which work is suspended — Bahá'ís gather for celebrations or commemorations, which are open to the public.

Because there are no clergy in the Bahá'í Faith, its work is voluntarily carried out by community members who contribute their time and energies to its development. Each local Bahá'í community is administratively governed by a nine-member local Spiritual Assembly, which is democratically elected each year. Communities also benefit from the advice and counsel of members of appointed institutions serving at the local through international levels. Bahá'ís do not organize themselves as "congregations" — choosing a group based on social or theological preferences. Rather, for administrative purposes, Bahá'ís organize themselves in geographically-based communities, according to civil boundaries, but strive to act at the neighborhood level for many activities.

The Bahá'í teachings emphasize the importance of personal initiative, responsibility, and focus in relation to the development of the community. The individual is free to decide in what ways he or she would like to support the activities of the community. One may well not be able to be personally involved in every type of community activity, but each person can find avenues for service suited to his or her interests and talents, as well as the local community's needs. As individuals offer their services through different core activities, a unified diversity of action is created within the community. In this way, rather than one or a few religious leaders serving the needs of a congregation of passive members, every individual becomes an active collaborator, adding his or her God-given talents to the task of building a spiritual society.

CHAPTER 6

Recognizing the Promised Age:
Expectation and Fulfillment

*Open the doors of your hearts. He Who
is the Spirit verily standeth before them.*

– BAHÁ'U'LLÁH

Expectation of the Promised Age

A striking, common thread running through the scriptures and traditions of the world's major religions is the anticipation of a promised age when peace and righteousness will prevail in the world. But these religious writings warn that before attaining the promised age of God, humanity will first experience a period of spiritual darkness that will be characterized by selfishness, hatred, violence, unethical conduct, and the decline of religion:

> And the people shall be oppressed, every one by another, and every one by his neighbour.... (Judaism)

> ∾

> ...people will be greedy, take to wicked behavior, will be merciless, indulge in hostilities without any cause, unfortunate, extremely covetous.... (Hinduism)

> ∾

The world will fall into promiscuity.... Among such humans, brethren, keen mutual enmity will become the rule, keen ill-will, keen animosity, passionate thoughts even of killing.... (Buddhism)

❧

...in the last days perilous times shall come. For men shall be lovers of their own selves, covetous, boasters, proud, blasphemers, disobedient to parents, unthankful, unholy, without natural affection, trucebreakers, false accusers, incontinent, fierce, despisers of those that are good, traitors, heady, highminded, lovers of pleasures more than lovers of God.... (Christianity)

❧

The religious leaders of that day will be the most evil religious leaders under the heavens; sedition and dissension will go out from them and to them will it return. (Islam)

The scriptures of the world's faiths promise, however, that humanity's dark hour will be followed by the light of peace, unity, and virtue:

...they shall beat their swords into plowshares, and their spears into pruninghooks: nation shall not lift up sword against nation, neither shall they learn war any more. (Judaism)

❧

The minds of the people will become pure as flawless crystal, and they will be as if awakened at the conclusion of a night. And these men, the residue of mankind, will thus be transformed.... (Hinduism)

❧

The people will all feel equal, and will be of one mind, mutually expressing pleasure upon meeting their fellows.... (Buddhism)

❧

And God shall wipe away all tears from their eyes; and there shall be no more death, neither sorrow, nor crying, neither shall there be any more pain: for the former things are passed away. (Christianity)

❧

And the earth shall shine with the light of her Lord.... (Islam)

Fulfillment of the Promised Age

Bahá'u'lláh has proclaimed that this is the age promised in past scriptures, when humanity is moving from the time of conflict, injustice, and materialism toward a period of peace, justice, and spirituality. He wrote:

> ...the break of the morn of divine guidance must...follow the darkness of the night of error. For this reason, in all chronicles and traditions reference hath been made unto these things, namely that iniquity shall cover the surface of the earth and darkness shall envelop mankind.

❧

The Day, promised unto you in all the Scriptures, is now come.

❧

Great indeed is this Day! The allusions made to it in all the sacred Scriptures as the Day of God attest its greatness.

The Bahá'í scriptures offer additional insights into how the world is moving from darkness to light. From the Bahá'í perspective, two processes are at work in the world today. One process is the decline and breakdown of an old order — social, economic, political, and religious — that is materialistic in its approach or is clinging to standards and practices that no longer meet the needs of the age. This process of disintegration is seen in wars, terrorism, moral confusion, and the inability of leaders to address society's problems. Bahá'u'lláh wrote: "The winds of despair are, alas, blowing from every direction, and the strife that divides and afflicts the human race is daily increasing. The signs of impending convulsions and chaos can now be discerned, inasmuch as the prevailing order appears to be lamentably defective."

The second process that is occurring in the world is the building up of a new social order based on spiritual principles, including the ideal of unity. In this process of integration, individuals and various groups promote moral values and strive to create new models of interaction that are cooperative and constructive.

The process of decline and disintegration is akin to the deterioration of a house whose foundations and supports have weakened — just as the structure of current society has been undermined by conflict, corruption, injustice, and abandonment of moral values. At the same time, increasing numbers of people are contributing to the process of growth — building a new house that rests on the solid foundation of unity, moral rectitude, justice, and spirituality. Both processes are occurring at once. As time passes, the defects and instability of the old house become more clear, and the solidity and security of the newly-emerging structure become more obvious.

According to the Bahá'í view, the long-promised age of peace and unity will not instantly and magically appear in the world. Rather, it will be gradually and increasingly manifest as a new, spiritually-based social order is established through great effort over a long period of time. Humanity will have to overcome many obstacles and learn through trial and experience that the solutions to the major problems in the world are fundamentally not political, economic, or social. Instead, at their root, the profound challenges facing humanity are spiritual in nature and will, therefore, require spiritual solutions. The key to positively transforming the world will be to educate large numbers of people about the spiritual purpose of life and to help people apply spiritual principles in their personal lives and in the life of society.

In this age, the spiritual education of humanity began when the Báb planted the seeds of a new way of life throughout Persia. That process gained momentum when, during Bahá'u'lláh's lifetime, the Bahá'í teachings spread to approximately a dozen countries, principally in the Middle East. It further accelerated during 'Abdu'l-Bahá's ministry as the Bahá'í Faith was established in nearly 20 more countries, including in Europe, North America, Australasia, and the Far East. By the early 1950's, the Bahá'í message had spread to more than 100 countries and territories in the East and the West. And by 1992, just a century after Bahá'u'lláh's passing, his Faith had been established in over 200 countries of the world and given rise to a community reflecting humanity's diversity.

Once the Bahá'í teachings had taken root in all corners of the globe, Bahá'ís began to develop an educational system that could train large numbers of people in Bahá'í spiritual principles and their practical application. In the 1990's, under the guidance of the Universal House of Justice, Bahá'í communities throughout the world started training programs consisting of a sequence of courses. These training classes, usually offered in small groups called study circles, combine study and service. In addition to learning about spiritual principles and their application, participants acquired the skills and qualities to positively contribute to the spiritual education of others. Through this training process, individuals could also learn how to educate children in character development and to encourage young teenagers to develop their moral identity and to offer their energies to building a better world.

This educational process has grown exponentially since it was first established. In 2001, within five years of the launch of the program, some 94,000 individuals worldwide had completed Bahá'í training classes. By 2006, that number had risen to nearly a quarter million people who had completed nearly 575,000 courses, and since then, the number of participants has continued to rise. Because this educational process is open to the public and is neighborhood-based, often taking place in homes, it allows large numbers of people to become active participants in building spiritually-based communities. Participants are welcome to take part in activities regardless of whether they have any interest in joining the Bahá'í Faith. Moreover, because the system is self-perpetuating — as more individuals are trained, more have the capacity to serve and to train others — it has shown the potential to reach ever-larger numbers of people around the world. This training process is expected to reach millions of people within the coming years. Therefore, the goal of offering spiritual education to humanity is not merely a fanciful hope, but is a practical reality that Bahá'ís are methodically and joyfully attempting to carry out.

As the educational process instituted by the worldwide Bahá'í community continues to grow, more people will commit themselves to living lives centered on spiritual principles and to developing local communities based on those same principles. In turn, moral values will begin to permeate those communities. As these local communities grow in human resources, they will increasingly tackle and solve social and economic problems through consultation and the application of spiritual principles. And as spiritual awareness begins to take hold and motivate more elements of society, laws and institutions will increasingly reflect the standards of justice and unity. Over time, humanity will see the emergence of a new civilization that will fulfill the promises of past ages.

Two factors will ensure that the goal of establishing a spiritual civilization will be realized. First, experimentation and learning are at the heart of the Bahá'í approach to addressing humanity's challenges. This approach involves a cycle of consulting about how spiritual principles may be applied to solve practical problems, taking action based on decisions reached through consultation, and reflecting on the results of the action. As the learning cycle is repeated, lessons emerge and solutions are discovered. Because the process is grounded in learning, progress is assured.

The second factor that will ensure that the Bahá'í Faith will achieve its ultimate aim of establishing a spiritual civilization is the Covenant of Bahá'u'lláh — the spiritual arrangements he left to preserve the integrity and unity of his Faith. In the past, disunity, division, and deviation from original teachings arose in the religion of God because of disagreements about such basic questions as who should lead and what to believe (*i.e.*, the authority of institutions, the authenticity of the scriptures, and the nature of interpretation). The provisions of Bahá'u'lláh's Covenant address these issues. In his lifetime, Bahá'u'lláh explicitly and in writing designated his successor and established an administrative order that would protect and lead his religion. On the question of the authenticity of the Bahá'í scriptures, only the writings of Bahá'u'lláh, the Báb, and 'Abdu'l-Bahá — in their own handwriting or as dictated and signed by them — are considered authentic; hearsay has no authority. Further, while individuals are encouraged to arrive at their own understanding of the Bahá'í writings and share them with others, these interpretations are not binding and cannot be imposed upon others. For more than a century, these provisions have preserved the integrity and unity of the Bahá'í Faith despite attempts to create division within it. In sum, Bahá'u'lláh has not only proclaimed that this is the day to "build anew the whole world," but has also provided the vision and means to do so.

The Promised Figure

In addition to predicting the advent of an age of peace and righteousness, the sacred scriptures of the world's major religions anticipate the appearance of a promised figure who will usher in that age:

> ...the excellency of Carmel and Sharon, they shall see the glory of the LORD, and the excellency of our God.... And the glory of the LORD shall be revealed, and all flesh shall see it together: for the mouth of the LORD hath spoken. (Judaism)

౮

> Whenever there is decay of righteousness,...and there is exaltation of unrighteousness, then I Myself come forth; for the protection of the good, for the destruction of evildoers, for the sake of firmly establishing righteousness, I am born from age to age. (Hinduism)

౮

> At that period, brethren, there will arise in the world an Exalted One named Mettayya..., abounding in wisdom and goodness, happy, with knowledge of the worlds, unsurpassed as a guide to mortals willing to be led, a teacher for gods and men, an Exalted One, a Buddha, even as I am now. (Buddhism)

౮

> I have yet many things to say unto you, but ye cannot bear them now. Howbeit when he, the Spirit of truth, is come, he will guide you into all truth: for he shall not speak of himself; but whatsoever he shall hear, that shall he speak.... (Christianity)

౮

> What can such expect but that God should come down to them overshadowed with clouds...? (Islam)

Bahá'u'lláh unequivocally claimed he was the promised one of the peoples of the world:

> He Whose advent hath been foretold in the heavenly Scriptures is come, could ye but understand it.

> ☙

> The Call of God hath been raised, and the light of His countenance hath been lifted up upon men.

> ☙

> That which ye were promised in the Kingdom of God is fulfilled. This is the Word which the Son veiled when He said to those around Him that at that time they could not bear it.... Verily the Spirit of Truth is come to guide you unto all truth.... The Comforter Whose advent all the scriptures have promised is now come that He may reveal unto you all knowledge and wisdom.

Bahá'u'lláh's role as the promised one of all ages will serve as a point of unity for the peoples of the world.

In inviting humanity to consider his challenging claim, Bahá'u'lláh does not ask for blind acceptance, but only fair-minded examination:

> Verily I say, this is the Day in which mankind can behold the Face, and hear the Voice, of the Promised One.... It behoveth every man to blot out the trace of every idle word from the tablet of his heart, and to gaze, with an open and unbiased mind, on the signs of His Revelation, the proofs of His Mission, and the tokens of His glory.

What is the standard of proof to be used in ascertaining the truth of Bahá'u'lláh's claim? Jesus Christ provided the standard for determining the truth of anyone claiming a divine message: "Ye shall know them by their fruits.... Even so every good tree bringeth forth good fruit; but a corrupt tree bringeth forth evil fruit. A good tree cannot bring forth evil fruit, neither can a corrupt tree bring forth good fruit." The "fruits" Bahá'u'lláh offers in support of his claim are his life, his teachings, and his words.

In examining Bahá'u'lláh's life, one may well consider questions such as the following: Was his knowledge innate, or was it acquired from others through schooling? Did Bahá'u'lláh seek wealth and earthly power, or did he forsake these to serve humanity? Did he choose a life of comfort and ease, or did he willingly undergo suffering to spread his teachings? And did Bahá'u'lláh's life reflect the godliness, virtue, and personal sacrifice that have characterized the lives of previous Manifestations of God?

As to Bahá'u'lláh's teachings, were the spiritual truths Bahá'u'lláh emphasized consistent with the religious teachings of the past? Were Bahá'u'lláh's principles (such as the oneness of humankind, the unity of religion, the harmony of science and religion, and the equality of men and women) current in the thinking of the Middle East in the 1800's (or even today), or were these principles unique and revolutionary in the East and the West at the time they were uttered? Has the truth of Bahá'u'lláh's principles been borne out by their increasing recognition and acceptance in modern society? Would further application of Bahá'u'lláh's teachings address the spiritual and social needs of humanity today?

With regard to the words of Bahá'u'lláh, do they reflect the same spirit as the sacred scriptures of the past? Have the predictions set forth in his writings been fulfilled? And, most importantly, have Bahá'u'lláh's words transformed the lives of those who have turned to them and united people previously separated by divisions of economic status, nationality, race, and religion?

A Bahá'í is anyone who has concluded that Bahá'u'lláh is the Manifestation of God for this age. While a full and detailed knowledge of his teachings is not required in order to become a Bahá'í, what is important — in addition to catching the spark of faith — is becoming basically informed about the Faith's three central figures and understanding that Bahá'u'lláh has revealed laws and an administrative order that are to be followed. There is no ritual associated with becoming a Bahá'í — only a personal commitment of the heart and mind. While in many countries new Bahá'ís complete an enrollment card for administrative purposes, what is most important is whether the individual believes in the truth of Bahá'u'lláh's message and is willing to strive to follow the spiritual path Bahá'u'lláh has laid out.

Bahá'u'lláh's Words to Edward Granville Browne

In 1890, Edward Granville Browne, a scholar from Cambridge University, visited Bahá'u'lláh in the Holy Land. Browne, who was one of the few Westerners to have met Bahá'u'lláh and the only one known to have left a written account of his experience, penned the following description of his experience:

> ...I found myself in a large apartment, along the upper end of which ran a low divan, while on the side opposite to the door were placed two or three chairs. Though I dimly suspected whither I was going and whom I was to behold (for no distinct intimation had been given to me), a second or two elapsed ere, with a throb of wonder and awe, I became definitely conscious that the room was not untenanted. In the corner where the divan met the wall sat a wondrous and venerable figure.... The face of him on whom I gazed I can never forget, though I cannot describe it. Those piercing eyes seemed to read one's very

soul; power and authority sat on that ample brow.... No need to ask in whose presence I stood, as I bowed myself before one who is the object of a devotion and love which kings might envy and emperors sigh for in vain!

A mild dignified voice bade me be seated, and then continued: "Praise be to God that thou hast attained!...Thou hast come to see a prisoner and an exile.... We desire but the good of the world and the happiness of the nations; yet they deem us a stirrer up of strife and sedition worthy of bondage and banishment.... That all nations should become one in faith and all men as brothers; that the bonds of affection and unity between the sons of men should be strengthened; that diversity of religion should cease, and differences of race be annulled — what harm is there in this?... Yet so it shall be; these fruitless strifes, these ruinous wars shall pass away, and the 'Most Great Peace' shall come.... Do not you in Europe need this also? Is not this that which Christ foretold?... Yet do we see your kings and rulers lavishing their treasures more freely on means for the destruction of the human race than on that which would conduce to the happiness of mankind... These strifes and this bloodshed and discord must cease, and all men be as one kindred and one family.... Let not a man glory in this, that he loves his country; let him rather glory in this, that he loves his kind...."

Such, as far as I can recall them, were the words which, besides many others, I heard from Behá [Bahá'u'lláh]. Let those who read them consider well with themselves whether such doctrines merit death and bonds, and whether the world is more likely to gain or lose by their diffusion.

RECOMMENDED READINGS AND RESOURCES

Recommended Readings

The following recommended readings offer additional information about the Bahá'í Faith. The primary sources listed here include some of the many volumes of the sacred and authoritative writings of the Faith. The secondary sources identified below explore various aspects of Bahá'í teachings and practice.

SELECT PRIMARY SOURCES

The Book of Certitude (Kitáb-i-Iqán)

The Book of Certitude is Bahá'u'lláh's most important doctrinal work. In it, he discusses the nature of God and of divine revelation, addresses the unity of the Manifestations of God, and explains how the barriers that have traditionally divided the religions can be overcome.

The Hidden Words of Bahá'u'lláh

This book is a collection of 153 brief utterances devoted to ethical and spiritual themes. The short, inspiring passages contained in this work are often used for personal, spiritual reflection and study.

Gleanings from the Writings of Bahá'u'lláh

This selection of the writings of Bahá'u'lláh addresses themes such as the day of God, the Manifestations of God, the soul and its immortality, peace, and the spiritual meaning of life. *Gleanings* provides a taste of Bahá'u'lláh's various writings.

Some Answered Questions

This work contains 'Abdu'l-Bahá's responses to questions posed by an American woman on numerous topics, including the nature and functions of the Manifestations of God, Christian themes, Biblical prophecies, the origin and conditions of human beings, and various philosophical and practical issues. Many of the explanations are brief and contain simple analogies that make profound topics accessible to readers.

God Passes By

God Passes By is Shoghi Effendi's historical survey of the outstanding events of the Bahá'í Faith's first century, from 1844 to 1944.

Bahá'í Prayers

This book is a compilation of prayers revealed by Bahá'u'lláh, the Báb, and 'Abdu'l-Bahá. It includes the Bahá'í Obligatory Prayers, as well as prayers for various purposes such as assistance with difficulties, children, healing, protection, and unity.

The above primary sources are available for free online at the Bahá'í Reference Library website (reference.bahai.org/en) or may be purchased through amazon.com, barnesandnoble.com, bahaibookstore.com, and many local bookstores.

SELECT SECONDARY SOURCES

The Proofs of Bahá'u'lláh's Mission

This book contains selections from the Bahá'í writings offering proofs and evidences in support of Bahá'u'lláh's claim to be the Manifestation of God for this age.

Bahá'u'lláh's Teachings on Spiritual Reality

This work presents Bahá'u'lláh's teachings on such spiritual themes as the quest for spirituality, the spiritual life, material and spiritual reality, the progress of the soul and the nature of the afterlife, and humanity's spiritual education.

The Essence of the Covenant: Features, History, and Implications

The Essence of the Covenant explores how the Bahá'í Faith has maintained its unity and integrity during the critical first century after the passing of its founder. This work discusses how Bahá'í institutions and principles have maintained the cohesiveness of the Bahá'í Faith and analyzes the succession of authority from Bahá'u'lláh to 'Abdu'l-Bahá to the Bahá'í administrative order.

The Path Toward Spirituality: Sacred Duties and Practices of the Bahá'í Life

This book offers a practical guide to the exercises essential for spiritual growth: prayer, meditation, study of the Bahá'í Faith, teaching, observance of divine laws and principles, material offerings, and service.

For the Betterment of the World

This booklet presents a summary of the worldwide Bahá'í community's approach to social and economic development. It offers descriptions of development projects that Bahá'ís are carrying out and the concepts and approaches underlying these efforts. This resource is also available online through www.bahai.org.

The above secondary sources are available through bahaibookstore.com or palabrapublications.com.

WEBSITES

bahai.org

This is the official, international website of the Bahá'í Faith.

bahaullah.org

This website presents a photographic narrative of the life of Bahá'u'lláh.

reference.bahai.org

This website offers free electronic copies of the sacred and authoritative writings of the Bahá'í Faith.

bahaibookstore.com

This is an online source for Bahá'í sacred writings, as well as books and music produced by Bahá'ís.

CONTACTING THE AUTHOR

Comments, questions, and suggestions may be emailed to bahaiteachings@gmail.com.

REFERENCES

CHAPTER 1

Advent of Divine Justice 17; *Dawn-Breakers* xxv *et seq.*, xxix, xliii-xliv; *Epistle* 12, 118; *Gleanings* 27, 49-50, 66, 70, 74, 79-80, 166, 217; *God Passes By* 139; John 1:14; 10:38; 14:6; *A History of the Intellectual Development of Europe*; *Issues Related to the Study of the Bahá'í Faith* #10; *Kitáb-i-Aqdas* 2, parag. 182; *Kitáb-i-Iqán* 97, 142, 176, 199, 240; *Lights of Guidance* 478; *Paris Talks* 26, 32; *Promulgation* 19, 54, 84-85, 105-06, 114, 126, 128, 151, 154, 168-69, 173, 341, 346-47, 364-66, 401, 403-04, 411-12, 437, 467; *Secret of Divine Civilization* 92-94; *Selections from the Writings of 'Abdu'l-Bahá* 10, 51-52; *Selections from the Writings of the Báb* 106; *Some Answered Questions* 18-22, 47-48, 74-75, 94, 165-66, 168, 222; *World Order* 102, 114-15.

CHAPTER 2

Arohanui 89; *Bahá'í World Faith* 382-83; *Bahá'u'lláh and the New Era* 131; Genesis 1:26; *Gleanings* 65, 68, 70-71, 77, 154-59, 161, 171, 276, 299; *Guidelines for Local Spiritual Assemblies* chap. 14, p. 12; *Hidden Words* Arabic #6; *Importance of Obligatory Prayer and Fasting* #1; *Kitáb-i-Iqán* 118, 120; *Lights of Guidance* 207, 210, 298, 327, 360, 505; *Paris Talks* 60-61, 86, 89, 92, 97-99; *Promulgation* 41, 47, 81, 166, 226, 295, 307, 335, 351, 403-04, 417-18, 465; Research Department Memorandum (March 28, 1996); *Selections from the Writings of 'Abdu'l-Bahá* 130, 177, 185, 190, 194; *Some Answered Questions* 79, 118-19, 186, 205, 224-25, 229, 241, 287.

CHAPTER 3

Advent of Divine Justice 40; *Bahá'í World* vol. VI, 485; *Century of Light* 11; *Compilation of Compilations* vol. II, 379; *Epistle* 14, 138; *Gleanings* 79-80, 164, 249-50, 286; *God Passes By* 218, 386-87; *Guidelines for Local Spiritual Assemblies* chap. 7, p. 8; *Hidden Words* Persian # 54; *History of Bahá'í Educational Efforts in Iran*; *Kitáb-i-Iqán* 164; *Lights of Fortitude* 396-97; *Lights of Guidance* 481; *Paris Talks* 41, 143, 151; *Promise of World Peace*; *Promulgation* 61, 63, 64, 107-08, 117, 127, 132, 135, 141, 180, 182, 291, 298, 300, 314-18, 434, 454; *Secret of Divine Civilization* 64-65, 109; *Selections from the Writings of 'Abdu'l-Bahá*

Chapter 4

Chapter 5

CHAPTER 6

Bahá'í World vol. XIII, 460-61; *Bhagavad Gita* 4:7-8; *Essence of the Covenant* 159, 186; *Five Year Plan, 2001-2006* 126; *Gleanings* 10-11, 100, 105, 314; *God Passes By* 378-79; *Introduction to Shi'i Islam* 168 (quoting hadith from Muhammad); Isaiah 2:4, 3:5, 35:2, 40:5; John 16:12-13; *Kitáb-i-Iqán* 31-32; *Koran* 2:206, 39:69; *Lights of Guidance* 69, 439; Matthew 7:16-18; *Messages from the Universal House of Justice, 1963-1986* 39; *Phenomenon of Religion* 244-45, 249, 252 (quoting *Bhagavata Purana* 12:3:24-25; *Dialogues of the Buddha* vol. 3, 70-71, 73-74; *Vishnu Purana* 4:24:25-9; *White Lotus-Maitreya Doctrine* 212); Rev. 21:4; 2 Timothy 3:1-4; *Selections from the Writings of 'Abdu'l-Bahá* 101; *Tablets of Bahá'u'lláh* 11, 244; *2002 Brittanica Book of the Year* 302; *A Traveller's Narrative* vol. II, Introduction, xxxix-xl; *World Order* 32, 104-05, 170.

BIBLIOGRAPHY

Works by the Authoritative Centers of the Bahá'í Faith

BAHÁ'U'LLÁH

———. *Epistle to the Son of the Wolf.* Wilmette, IL: Bahá'í Publishing Trust, 1988.

———. *Gleanings from the Writings of Bahá'u'lláh.* Wilmette, IL: Bahá'í Publishing Trust, 1983.

———. *Hidden Words.* Wilmette, IL: Bahá'í Publishing Trust, 1990.

———. *Kitáb-i-Aqdas: The Most Holy Book.* Haifa: Bahá'í World Centre, 1992.

———. *Kitáb-i-Iqán: The Book of Certitude.* Wilmette, IL: Bahá'í Publishing Trust, 1989.

———. *Prayers and Meditations.* Wilmette, IL: Bahá'í Publishing Trust, 1987.

———. *Summons of the Lord of Hosts.* Haifa: Bahá'í World Centre, 2002.

———. *Tablets of Bahá'u'lláh.* Wilmette, IL: Bahá'í Publishing Trust, 1988.

———. *Tabernacle of Unity.* [Haifa]: Bahá'í World Centre, 2006.

THE BÁB

———. *Selections from the Writings of the Báb.* Haifa: Bahá'í World Centre, 1982.

'ABDU'L-BAHÁ

———. *Paris Talks.* 10th ed. London: Bahá'í Publishing Trust, 1961.

———. *Promulgation of Universal Peace.* 2nd ed. Wilmette, IL: Bahá'í Publishing Trust, 1982.

———. *Secret of Divine Civilization.* Wilmette, IL: Bahá'í Publishing Trust, 1990.

——. *Selections from the Writings of 'Abdu'l-Bahá.* Haifa: Bahá'í World Centre, 1982.

——. *Some Answered Questions.* Wilmette, IL: Bahá'í Publishing Trust, 1985.

——. *Tablets of the Divine Plan.* Wilmette, IL: Bahá'í Publishing Trust, 1993.

——. *Will and Testament of 'Abdu'l-Bahá.* Wilmette, IL: Bahá'í Publishing Trust, 1944.

SHOGHI EFFENDI

——. *Advent of Divine Justice.* Wilmette, IL: Bahá'í Publishing Trust, 1984.

——. *Arohanui: Letters from Shoghi Effendi to New Zealand.* Suva, Fiji Islands: Bahá'í Publishing Trust, 1982.

——. *Bahá'í Administration.* Wilmette, IL: Bahá'í Publishing Trust, 1968.

——. *Faith of Bahá'u'lláh: A World Religion.* Wilmette, IL: Bahá'í Publishing Committee, n.d. (reprint from *World Order Magazine,* vol. XIII, no. 7, October 1947).

——. *God Passes By.* Rev. ed. Wilmette, IL: Bahá'í Publishing Trust, 1979.

——. *Unfolding Destiny: Messages from the Guardian of the Bahá'í Faith to the Bahá'í Community of the British Isles.* London: Bahá'í Publishing Trust, 1981.

——. *World Order of Bahá'u'lláh: Selected Letters.* 2nd rev. ed. Wilmette, IL: Bahá'í Publishing Trust, 1982.

——. *World Religion: A Summary of Its Aims, Teachings, and History* (reprinted as Appendix III in Root, Martha L. *Tahirih the Pure.* Los Angeles: Kalimát Press, 1981).

THE UNIVERSAL HOUSE OF JUSTICE

——. *Four Year Plan: Messages of the Universal House of Justice.* Riviera Beach, FL: Palabra Publications, 1996.

——. *Issues Related to the Study of the Bahá'í Faith: Extracts from Letters Written on behalf of the Universal House of Justice.* Wilmette, IL: Bahá'í Publishing Trust, 1999.

——. *Messages from the Universal House of Justice: 1963-1986, The Third Epoch of the Formative Age.* Wilmette, IL: Bahá'í Publishing Trust, 1996.

——. *Promise of World Peace.* Wilmette, IL: Bahá'í Publishing Trust, 1985.

———. *Turning Point: Selected Messages of the Universal House of Justice and Supplementary Material, 1996-2006*. West Palm Beach, FL: Palabra Publications, 2006.

———. Unpublished letter: Riḍván 150 (1993).

———. Unpublished Memorandum of the Research Department of the Universal House of Justice: March 28, 1996 (quoting 'Abdu'l-Bahá).

———. *Wellspring of Guidance: Messages, 1963-1968*. Rev. ed. Wilmette, IL: Bahá'í Publishing Trust, 1976.

———. *A Wider Horizon: Selected Messages of the Universal House of Justice: 1983-1992*. Riviera Beach, FL: Palabra Publications, 1992.

Compilations of Bahá'í Writings

———. *Bahá'í Education: A Compilation of Extracts from the Bahá'í Writings*. 2nd rev. ed. London: Bahá'í Publishing Trust, 1998.

———. *Bahá'í Meetings/The Nineteen Day Feast: Extracts from the Writings of Bahá'u'lláh, 'Abdu'l-Bahá, and Shoghi Effendi*. Wilmette, IL: Bahá'í Publishing Trust, 1976.

———. *Bahá'í Prayers: A Selection of Prayers Revealed by Bahá'u'lláh, the Báb, and 'Abdu'l-Bahá*. Wilmette, IL: Bahá'í Publishing Trust, 2002.

———. *Bahá'í World Faith: Selected Writings of Bahá'u'lláh and 'Abdu'l-Bahá*. 2nd ed. Wilmette, IL: Bahá'í Publishing Trust, 1956.

———. *Bahá'u'lláh's Teachings on Spiritual Reality*. Riviera Beach, FL: Palabra Publications, 1996.

———. *Compilation of Compilations*. Vol. I. Maryborough, Victoria, Australia: Bahá'í Publications Australia, 1991.

———. *Compilation of Compilations*. Vol. II. Maryborough, Victoria, Australia: Bahá'í Publications Australia, 1991.

———. *Consultation*. Rev. ed. London: Bahá'í Publishing Trust, 1990.

———. *Guidelines for Local Spiritual Assemblies*. Rev. Evanston, IL: National Spiritual Assembly of the Bahá'ís of the United States, 2010.

———. *Importance of Deepening our Knowledge and Understanding of the Faith*. Thornhill, Ontario: Bahá'í Community of Canada, 1983.

———. *Importance of Obligatory Prayer and Fasting*, May 2000. http://bahai-library.com/compilations/obligatory.prayer.html.

———. *Lights of Guidance: A Bahá'í Reference File*. 3rd rev. ed. New Delhi, India: Bahá'í Publishing Trust, 1994.

——. *Principles of Bahá'í Administration.* Manchester: Bahá'í Publishing Trust, 1950.

——. *Proofs of Bahá'u'lláh's Mission.* 2nd ed. Riviera Beach, FL: Palabra Publications, 1995.

——. *Selected Guidance Concerning Devotional Gatherings*, Sept. 19, 2001. http://bahai-library.com/uhj/devotional.meetings.html.

Other Sources

Alcohol and Injury in Emergency Departments: Summary of the Report from the WHO Collaborative Study on Alcohol and Injuries. France: World Health Organization, 2007.

Bahá'í Faith 1844-1963 Information Statistical & Comparative. Israel, n.d.

Bahá'í International Community.

——. *Bahá'u'lláh.* Plantation, FL: Spiritual Assembly of the Bahá'ís of Plantation, FL, 1992.

——. *Century of Light.* [Haifa]: Bahá'í World Centre, 2001.

——. *For the Betterment of the World.* New York: Bahá'í International Community, 2003.

Bahá'í World.

——. Vol. VI. Wilmette, IL: Bahá'í Publishing Trust, 1980.

——. Vol. XIII. Haifa: Universal House of Justice, 1980.

Balyuzi, H.M.

——. *'Abdu'l-Bahá: The Centre of the Covenant of Bahá'u'lláh.* 2nd ed. Oxford: George Ronald, 1987.

——. *Báb, The: The Herald of the Day of Days.* Oxford: George Ronald, 1974.

——. *Bahá'u'lláh: The King of Glory.* Oxford: George Ronald, 1980.

Besant, Annie (trans.). *Bhagavad Gita.* Madras, India: Theosophical Publishing House, 1939.

Browne, Edward G. *A Traveller's Narrative Written to Illustrate the Episode of the Báb.* Vol. II, Introduction. Cambridge: Cambridge University Press Warehouse, 1891.

Draper, John William. 2nd ed. *A History of the Intellectual Development of Europe.* New York: Harper & Brothers, Publishers, 1864.

Esslemont, J.E. *Bahá'u'lláh and the New Era.* 4th rev. ed. Wilmette, IL: Bahá'í Publishing Trust, 1980.

Hanson, Glen R., *et al.*, *Drugs and Society*. 10th ed. Sudbury, MA: Jones and Bartlett Publishers, 2009.

Harper, Barron. *Lights of Fortitude: Glimpses into the Lives of the Hands of the Cause of God*. Oxford: George Ronald, 1997.

History of Bahá'í Educational Efforts in Iran. http://denial.bahai.org/003.php.

Holy Bible. King James Version. Nashville, TN: Thomas Nelson Publishers, 1984.

Honnold, Annamarie (ed.). *Vignettes from the Life of 'Abdu'l-Bahá*. Oxford: George Ronald, 1986.

International Teaching Centre. *Five Year Plan, 2001-2006: Summary of Achievements and Learning*. [Haifa]: Bahá'í World Centre, 2006.

Ives, Howard Colby. *Portals to Freedom*. Oxford: George Ronald, 1953.

Ministry of the Custodians: 1957-1963, An Account of the Stewardship of the Hands of the Cause. Haifa: Bahá'í World Centre, 1992.

Momen, Moojan.

—— (ed.). *Bábí and Bahá'í Religions, 1844-1944: Some Contemporary Western Accounts*. Oxford: George Ronald, 1981.

——. *An Introduction to Shi'i Islam*. Oxford: George Ronald, 1985.

——. *Phenomenon of Religion: A Thematic Approach*. Oxford: Oneworld Publications, 1999.

Morrison, Gayle. *To Move the World*. Wilmette, IL: Bahá'í Publishing Trust, 1982.

Nabíl-i-A'zam. *The Dawn-Breakers: Nabíl's Narrative of the Early Days of the Bahá'í Revelation*. Wilmette, IL: Bahá'í Publishing Trust, 1996.

Rodwell, J.M. *The Koran*. Charleston, SC: BiblioBazaar, 2008.

Taherzadeh, Adib. *The Revelation of Bahá'u'lláh: Baghdad 1853-63*. Vol. 1. Rev. ed. Oxford: George Ronald, 1992.

2002 Brittanica Book of the Year. Chicago: Encyclopedia Brittanica, 2002.

Vafai, Shahin.

——. *Essence of the Covenant: Features, History, and Implications*. West Palm Beach, FL: Palabra Publications, 2005.

——. *Path Toward Spirituality: Sacred Duties and Practices of the Bahá'í Life*. 2nd ed. Riviera Beach, FL: Palabra Publications, 1998.